Smart Cities

Series Editor
Jean-Charles Pomerol

Smart Cities

Reality or Fiction

Claude Rochet

WILEY

First published 2018 in Great Britain and the United States by ISTE Ltd and John Wiley & Sons, Inc.

ISTE Ltd
27–37 St George's Road
London SW19 4EU
UK

www.iste.co.uk

John Wiley & Sons, Inc.
111 River Street
Hoboken, NJ 07030
USA

www.wiley.com

Library of Congress Control Number: 2018949416

British Library Cataloguing-in-Publication Data
A CIP record for this book is available from the British Library
ISBN 978-1-78630-299-1

Contents

Foreword

Inhabiting, Moving, Working, Meeting, Playing, Living at Last ...

Everything seems to indicate that the fourth economy, the economy of cities – the one which will eventually follow the agricultural era, the industrial period and the digital age – will raise questions surrounding human life, focusing on quality rather than quantity and we will stop believing that just because we are technically able to do something, means we necessarily should!

Everything seems to indicate that this fourth economy will not arise painlessly, without sacrifice or without transformations. The most important thing lies in giving up social constructionism which sees man as the product of his available technology and rights. Take geography out of the equation, forget about history, ignore the environment, culture and language, give a group of humans the systems and resources that will ensure their survival and you will get a town. Maybe. A smart town? Most likely. A society? Certainly not, what an idea! In fact, we already know full well: society doesn't exist!

If you have a problem with the city, if you think you have a problem with society, see a shrink! There is no collective issue that cannot be turned into individual guilt! There is no social question that a solid network of systems cannot answer! Since there is no society, there is no city either, all there is the forced compact coexistence of isolated individuals – connected, yet alone. There will never be a city again, since cities used to be physical meeting grounds, places of forced intimacy between thousands of souls, now that their constant connection and their fascination for digital screens separate them so intensely.

And everything seems to indicate that the fourth economy will be violently at odds with some of our most hammered in and commonly accepted truths, some of the most widely believed ideas, a few of the highest erudite MBAs that will have served to spread confusion and cynicism while wasting energy resources throughout two or three decades. Among them will be misconceptions wielded by managerial literature, the compulsive need to rely on digital technology, the dogmas of systemic individualism and its programed liberations.

When the French Council of State, in February 2018, published a memo advising they adapt France's laws and society to digital technology, we all understood that "when all you have is a hammer, everything looks like a nail" – and that the Council of State is keeping up with current trends, in this case, insignificance. And not only that but also the idea that intelligence lies in systems and their applications, that a society is the sum of the people within it, or that a city is smart because its people are smart. The magic of cities – and their mystery – is that it takes a bit of everything for one to succeed, and that a city eventually eludes the plans, programs and systems that are made for it. Somewhere, somehow, cities are free.

Living, playing, moving, meeting are central to these separations, these gaps and this invention.

Cities have these vital functions in spades and even claim to hold more than that, meet, play, self-actualize, for example. Cities are icons of modernism, they stand as the dreams of everyone who felt left out, the people forgotten by the government and modernism's great machine. They are a liberation to all those still living in villages, with churches and cobbled streets. They are the lead blanket of judgmental gazes of all against all. Cities are the epicenters for the reinvention of knowledge and all things common, of the will to live for the century to come.

Cities as self-designed mirrors of a modernism that does not resemble what was designed, does not respond to the demands of what its generous donators expected it to be – as a factory of the client, the crucible of people above ground, as organization of consent, obedience and shock at how much was promised.

Claude Rochet has dedicated a new volume to explaining what a smart city should and should not be. Nourished by various experiences, of projects and conferences that took him from Siberia to Namibia and from Casa Blanca in Mexico to Casablanca in Morocco, this book should be read by anyone with questions surrounding the city of tomorrow, on their living conditions, and who want to do something – and not just suffer in silence. It falls within a growing trend that refuses technical determinism, and intends to save the city from functionalism and constructivism.

It participates in the wholesome activity of de-radicalizing modernism, a new kind of fundamentalism, one that claims far more victims than any other, in the name of rampant progress.

What Claude Rochet writes must be read, meditated upon and applied by anyone confronted with questions about cities, space and territory. His first message is an invitation to come back to reality. A city is first and foremost a history and a geographical territory, and second, a system of sub-systems, an assembly of functions, a relayed network. It is an invitation to territorial intelligence, the delicate and profound fruit of knowledge of the reasons of human settlement, of local singularities, of collective preferences, of age-old teachings and of invisible continuous adaptations.

How recklessly our city-makers neglect, move or destroy techniques and methods with centuries' worth of experience behind them! Cities have reasons that go beyond financial considerations, means of communication, or even political determination. Rediscovering these often forgotten reasons, analyzing them, weighing their relevance and permanence, is often a way for urban planners and developers alike to make the right choices and select the appropriate tone.

A city is also an asset. Granted, but what kind? A material asset made of infrastructures and buildings, systems of connected networks and telecommunications count far less than the immaterial aspect made of collective intelligence, accumulated adaptations, and also rules of life, social practices, morals and traditions. Elements inherent to urbanism, which dictate that within a few kilometers, two Italian, Chinese or French cities will have different accents, perfumes, colors, all serving to create the surprise, the discovery, the intimacy of a city, elude all calculations, management models and functional systems; yet it is much more and much better, making cities unique and incomparable. And don't only think of

Florence or Pisa, Nice and Marseilles, think Tucson and Albuquerque, Puebla or Oaxaca, Xiamen or Wuhan!

The evidence that is outlined by Claude Rochet is that there is no point to a smart city; the point is to make its inhabitants smarter. Intelligent, meaning closer to their territory and to life; more open to the world and what matters to the world; more attentive to what cannot be bought or sold, to these minuscule and delicious singularities, that make the whole difference between one city and another, and make the flavor and the happiness of the "here", the "now" and the inter-self. This is because urban intelligence is also this sense of the limits which distinguishes, separates and abandons – conversely to the missteps of open societies, multicultural societies and above ground cities. The idiocy of those selling attractiveness, measures of creative classes, indicators of ethnic, sexual and cultural diversity only to subsequently admit they were recreating ghettos and replacing all old determinations by another, more modern one: money, should be cause for reflection among our representatives that are so often led to sacrifice to the myth of attractiveness and deliver territories to bounty hunters and subsidy-seeking drifters!

A city is a place of life. A place where women and men live and feel alive. They are its narrators, the city is their life. Not the search for investment capital, for the best techniques available or information system designers! Claude Rochet provides a number of examples of these perfect plans, of these impeccable programs, which only lack one thing: life, people and everything we call character, uniqueness, flesh and sentiment.

It is the most common and costly of mistakes; ignoring what makes a city outside of any plans, programs or invested capital. It is a question of size, no doubt. However, it is also a question of urbanism. Most importantly, however, it is a question of territorial intelligence, of respect for history, identity, morals and walks of life. Furthermore, unpredictability, surprise, free spaces, misappropriations and misuse. A city for living, without boredom. Therefore, perfect abstraction, appropriately executed contracts and flawless systems.

A city is freedom. How many of us have dreamt of the big city as a way of escaping the boredom of the countryside, the "what will people think?", the conformity forced by the neighborhood, the street, the neighbors? Cities ensure anonymity, no doubt. They ensure one gets lost in every sense of the word. They are also places that multiply interactions, they ensure no one can remain alone unless they choose to. Cities are places where solitude is a choice. Illusion or reality? At the time when the UK is appointing a Minister for loneliness, to fight modernism's first pathology, it is worth asking the question. Do cities have the solutions to the problems caused by cities?

Here, we are pitting city against city. City of encounters, of possibilities, unpredictability, surprises, against the city of plans, programs and systems. In sum, the city used by people as opposed to the city as a service, the lived in city against all the systems that make a city a city. No, a city is not a business just like any other, a brand like any other and a product like any other.

And this is what we call living, inhabiting, getting around, working, etc. in a complicit city, a city that is friendly and caring. Far from the systems of systems and their totalitarian grip, far from the city created by the like of Google, Amazon or any other current manifestation of the privatization of all common goods and the liquidation of all that made life easy and good, hence it is necessary to integrate cities and their surrounding territories – such as fields, deserts, forests, without which they would not be cities. Thus, there is a need to conduct a study on real diversity which arises from the internal unity of a population, which makes a city a community, entirely like no other. And thus, lastly, the need for a new humanist approach to building cities and thinking about them – humanism such as modesty, respect, care of knowledge and interests before it, and which remains out of reach of the manipulators of reality, identity, pride and bond.

Hervé JUVIN

Introduction

Our representatives, administrators, citizens, entrepreneurs, and so on are today beset by the idea of smart cities which compels us to deploy digital networks that should provide us with the solution to all current urban development problems: pollution, clean energies, lives facilitated through security which could be provided by data centers and their crime and catastrophe-predicting algorithms. Some technical experts prophesize a new industrial revolution which will be based on the Internet (Klaus Schwab) and others (Jeremy Rifkin) see the third based on energy. When the topic of smart cities comes up, it is generally in reference to cities where costly investments in digital technologies help improve traffic, manage energy flows and transport, and improve management decisions using data processing.

One of the many contradictions and pitfalls of this approach is forgetting that a city constitutes a system of interdependent sub-systems. The IT industry is by far the greediest in terms of energy per unit of production, and it utilizes rare minerals already in danger of depletion that are unevenly spread out across the planet, which incurs as many geopolitical risks as oil does. Before even the oil crisis reaches its peak, we are already in the process of depleting the existing metals [BIH 10]! As formulated today, the two objectives of the smart city – a supposed intelligence provided by digital technology and the cure for energy waste – are contradictory: its technological substrate consumes more energy than it is supposed to save [LAP 17].

The objective of this book is to allow the reader to recap on this subject without going in depth into the techniques and the underlying scientific fundamentals that are generally well explained in the specialist literature and will be abundantly referenced throughout the document. The idea is to present a way of approaching cities that is rooted in the history of urban development and integrates the economic, social, political and technological components of cities as a *system of living* into a *system of systems*, integrating heterogeneous systems which each have their own logic and their own dynamic, their own associated abilities and their own inherent challenges. It is intentionally concise, especially considering the scope of the subject. It is aimed at a reader who is not a theorist and even less an expert, but needs a few theoretical pointers to enlighten his or her work. It illustrates these points using concrete experiences.

To the administrator, the representative and the citizen, it proposes the basis for an integrative line of thinking which avoids the pitfall of reducing a set to its sub-set: a city is not *just* its economy, its culture, traffic, energy, housing, etc. but it is the integration of all of these elements. To the entrepreneur, it offers a perspective on their activity that likens it to a rock in an edifice which is bigger than him or her, a great creation that inspires and draws them in and gives them meaning. To the citizen, it offers a path to reconstructing the link between a common good and an individual one which was the basis for the prosperity of medieval towns and cities.

Chapter 1 presents the decoding of this concept of smart cities and its pitfalls. As with the advent of computing and the Internet, the arrival of a new technology is cluttered by a discourse which blends technical elements, lyricism, ideology, and often propaganda, faced with which the client – in this case, the citizen – must be able to discern and not fall victim to what Belarusian essayist Evgueny Morozov [MOR 13] called *"To save everything, click here"*. A technology is a tool serving an end, especially when its power allows us to imagine new ends, and, conversely, we must not hold said technology responsible for the way that some misuse it, least of all its promoters. If one hits their finger with a hammer, it is not the hammer's fault, but rather that person's own incompetence. Throughout this book, we will be presenting methods for the reader to avoid the pitfalls of "solutionism" which Morozov describes in great detail, including the argument often made by technology promoters that present them as "solutions" to problems which do not exist. We should not be expecting problems to conform to the seller's solutions, but rather for the solution to solve the buyer's problem … on condition that the latter be able to present it correctly, which is not necessarily in the seller's best interest, who in the short term is better served dealing with an ignorant buyer who is likely to fall under the charm of technological lyricism, if not under that of some technical experts – the danger of which we will give a glimpse later on.

Chapter 2 sets the scene on smart cities: urban growth will mainly concern the developing world. The urban population will increase there where, as in sub-Saharan Africa, a demographic transition has not yet occurred and where the standard of living is going to rise without the possibility of a simple reproduction of the mode of growth and of energy consumption as in the West. The energy issue is thus becoming essential in the design of the smart city, but we must not become deluded over the contribution of renewable energies, which are often intermittent and can remain very polluting depending on their means of generation. We are far from being able to leave behind the age of fossil fuels and the environmental and geopolitical problems they pose. Nonetheless, the age of the smart city is introducing geopolitical ruptures with a tipping of the world's polarity back towards the East and the South, and managerial, technological and scientific breakthroughs with the appearance of the new sciences of cities.

Chapter 3 defines smart cities in regard to the state of the art of new sciences of the city, or a structure of *systems of systems*. These systems obey different principles of modeling: the physical systems (transport, energy, waste, etc.) can be modeled using measurable values that obey the laws of physics and human systems rest upon the behaviors of humans which can neither be measured nor predicted by the laws of physics. The designer and manager of a smart city must therefore be able to navigate this multidisciplinarity of approaches and integrate these various systems to make a new art of urbanism similar to what the keystone did to medieval architecture.

Chapter 4 presents the design methods for smart cities as a complex system which forms the *new sciences of cities*. We can now identify the laws of urban development, applicable no matter the context, which will allow us to comprehend in each individual case why a city became unintelligent and with which tools it would be possible to redirect it. There is an optimal size for a city beyond which its complexity becomes out of control and it becomes easier to reason in terms of clusters of medium-sized cities rather than megacities, which is what the Chinese now do. A city does not follow a predefined pattern, but is an *emergence:* it has traits which only appear through the interaction of sub-systems among one another. The possibility of being able to "age well in the city" is the result of the interaction between systems, such as housing, transport, public health and social life. If the problem of aging is common to all cities, its solution will rely on integrating rules about how we treat old folk in each culture and civilization.

Chapter 5 presents a smart city in action. We will present the strategies of urban development used in Singapore (a smart city designed as such from the beginning in order to move a poor nation to the rank of rich nation), Russia (where the strategy of monotowns is the basis for a transitional policy towards an innovative economy of the Third Industrial Revolution), Copenhagen (a city designed on the human scale), Christchurch (a city rebuilt using the expression of the needs of its inhabitants as a condition for its resilience), Casablanca and others. We will also see a few specific points that a city must address which will allow it to build what its intelligence must become: energy management, waste management, transport management, the use of digital technology and their dangers (the famous *Big Data!*), the possibility of local currencies thanks to cryptocurrencies and which political organization could govern a smart city.

In the backdrop: a new industrial revolution?

The argument of a new industrial revolution is often brought up in justifying the relevance of policies promoting *smart cities*. If there really is an industrial revolution, it is only really the second phase of the Third Industrial Revolution based on information technologies which we can trace back to the mid-1970s when the expansion of computing began to make data-processing a generic technology in economic progress and the transformation of businesses. In place of the mass production model of the Second Industrial Revolution, vertical and standardized, a new model appeared favoring satellite businesses and smaller production units rather than the giant factories of the era of mass production. The Internet of Things (which connects not only humans but also objects among one another and objects to humans) helped create configurations at the organizational level (sometimes referred to as business 4.0 [IDC 16]), and also cities that were much more agile which could remedy the negative externalities of a mode of development based on fossil fuels, megacities and their consequences: pollution, energy waste, stress and multiple health risks associated with our current way of living in large cities.

What is the real difference? Industrial revolutions have constant traits, one of which is the lyricism towards the merits of technology which should signal an era of generalized progress. This was the case for the First

Industrial Revolution based on coal and the second based on electricity and oil: we now know what ended up happening. There was an industrial revolution upon the appearance of a new technology causing a leap in productivity. This was the case with coal, chemistry, electricity, fossil fuels and then computing. This change affected all of society, business structures, social relations and national strategies, employment qualifications, their hierarchies, salaries, and so on. The point that all these mutations have in common is that they occur in cycles: an ascending cycle is characterized by growing returns, and then a descending cycle is characterized by diminishing returns. Economic history since the beginning of the industrial era is a succession of technological cycles each lasting approximately 50 years and including a growth phase and a decline phase[1].

We are currently within the phase of diminishing returns for fossil fuels and the whole production model of the Second Industrial Revolution. The first wave of the Third Industrial Revolution based on information technologies has experienced the period of 1.0, with the automation of processes, and of 2.0, with transaction computing which interacts with the users; we are now entering the realm of 3.0 – or 4.0 for the more enthusiastic, which integrates objects into transactions: the Internet of Things (IoT). All of the business organization models and beyond the cities are involved.

We are seeing a convergence between the proliferation of a new generation of information technologies and the end of a growth cycle based on fossil fuels. In addition, pollution and the cost of waste management are reaching unsustainable peaks, in particular in the large cities of the world. Pollution is not a new phenomenon and has never prevented polluters from polluting, but what is new is that what is known as "the green economy" is now becoming viable, the industry of renewable growth is now entering a phase of growing returns while polluting growth is now in a phase of diminishing returns: industrial development economists, Erik Reinert and John Matthews, look at this and see the beginning of the second technological cycle of the Third Industrial Revolution [REI 15]. What is new is not the sudden appearance of an "environmental conscience" which would make pollution, in particular the pollution of rich countries being exported to poor countries, unsustainable, but the green economy is an economy of increasing returns: it is now viable to invest in green growth. The Chinese

---

1 For a more detailed analysis of the cycle of industrial revolutions see [ROC 15a].

have understood this perfectly: they are transforming the disadvantage of having the most polluted cities by investing in clean energy innovations.

Let us not confuse *green economy* and *renewable energies*. What Erik Reinert and John Matthews refer to is the *industry* of green economy which has the signs of a new technological cycle, i.e. a continuous progression on the learning curve and incremental flows of innovations in the industry which considerably decrease the costs. This was the case for computing, where its economy really took off after the first petrol crisis in 1973 and developed according to Moore's law, meaning a constant increase in processing power and an equivalent decrease in prices. The computing industry from that day forward entered a cycle of increasing returns and diminishing costs. However, computing only became affordable from a user standpoint in the mid-1990s when the phenomenon known as "the Solow computer paradox" disappeared. This paradox states that when the productivity is correlated to investments in the computer industry, this correlation was negative until then.

We are at this point today with renewable energies. Unlike what certain buzzword speeches held by politicians and journalists may say, these energies have not reached their level of viability. To this day, we are still waiting for a technological advance which will help resolve the problem of storing electricity. For the International Energy Agency (IEA), the prediction is an adoption level of renewables close to 15% on the horizon for 2040. We are far from the outlandish statements made by the French minister of the environment who, in 2014, stated that solar energy would represent 10% of the world's electricity, when it in fact only makes up 0.8%.

Digital transition, environmental transition and unsustainability of the urban model are all combining. In addition, there is a demographic transition with a large growth in urban population still to come, especially in developing countries. The energy transition and the proliferation of this new wave of technology create opportunities that economic players such as governments may or may not have picked up on in more or less biased ways.

Then, the early 21st Century saw the entrance of this concept of "smart cities" …

What Do We Mean by "Smart City" and Where Does This Idea Come From?

Three names are to be remembered: Songdo, Masdar and Plan IT Valley.

The city of Songdo, in Korea, was developed by an American company in partnership with a steel-making company called Posco and a company called Cisco with a budget of 40 billion dollars. The city received cutting-edge digital technologies provided by Cisco and is presented as being "100% connected". The people can work out with their online coaches, commercials will adapt depending on who is watching them, and all access points use biometric scanning. Close behind is Masdar in Abu Dhabi which cost 22 billion dollars. It is a city designed to hold 40,000 people and appears as a cluster of technologies that manage most limitations of a city built on a desert: energy production, water, climate control, integrated transport that removes the need for automobiles, etc. And lastly, we have *Plan IT Valley* in Portugal for an investment of 10 billion dollars, which hopes to hold 225,000 people. Financed by Cisco, Microsoft and a British engineering company, it is meant to provide an archetype for an entirely connected urban system able to manage all connected spaces and networkable activity.

The problem is that none of these cities are lived in, other than Songdo, and even then, far less than it was originally hoped. These are cities designed for rich people where there are no poor, sick or old people and no delinquency. These cities were created in total disconnect with any existing territory, and they have no history and inherited culture. They are mostly showcases for technologies that propose an optimization model for all urban flows such as traffic, energy, information, etc. through an integrated data-processing system that monitors all information. The most accomplished of such systems is Rio de Janeiro, designed by IBM for 14 billion dollars. This center is not an innovation in the sense where it would change city management as a whole. All it does is collect the data from 30 administrative services in the city. It improves decision making, in terms of quality and efficiency, but does nothing to change the nature of the fundamental problems encountered by a city [GAF 16]. It has no impact on solving Rio's fundamental problems, such as poverty, crime, *favelas* that are constantly growing, pollution: it simply automates what already exists. The city of Rio definitely manages all of this faster and more efficiently, but whether or not it manages it in a smarter fashion is a whole other matter, a political matter which goes beyond the realm of ability of a machine, regardless of how powerful it is, contrary to what the mainstream would suggest.

Figure 1.1. *The operations center of Rio de Janeiro, constructed by IBM*

The prominent actors in these realizations are IBM, Cisco and Siemens. These are "global companies", "solution integrators" who integrate machines and software to offer high-end solutions such as *Cokpit 15* by Siemens which aggregates all information produced by a city's processes into one same decision-making system. A similar type of product is IBM's *Operations Center software suite*. Other companies such as Samsung, Intel, Philips and Hitachi offer product line-ups for smart-city solutions. These businesses are the root of this conversation surrounding smart cities.

1.1. Not-so-smart smart cities!

As Adam Greenfield [GRE 13] explains it in his book *Against the Smart Cities*, this situation could correspond to the situation if designing the cities of the 20th Century had been granted to Bouygues, Roux-Combaluzier and Renault: concrete, towers and cars (and as we will see, that was the case to a certain extent). Each one of these companies reduces the city to what it knows how to do ...and sell. Thus, for Cisco, a leader in digital networking, a smart city is defined as *"the continuous integration of private and public services provided through a network of infrastructures to individuals, administrations and businesses"*.

Songdo, Masdar and Plan IT Valley are cities that were deliberately created with no territorial considerations, with no past, history, inherited culture and no interactions with their environment other than digital data exchanges. Nothing in the design of these cities takes into account what a city really is as a system of life. The latter is reduced to a technical system that is supposedly reliable, lifeless and impervious to the hazards and unpredictability of human behavior. When we take a look at the conversation surrounding smart cities as Greenfield has, we see that these cities do not live in the present. A sociologist would have a hard time studying its inhabitants, what their social codes are, their myths, their rituals and their founding taboos, and the specifics of this city. Their history is reduced to the promise of a *new age* future provided by technology. Social life is reduced to a perpetually aspiring technology that promises a perfect world. The city is inhabited by an archetype of the perfect family: average education, two children, standardized workplaces, perfect transportation systems that never break down, a city without poor, old or disabled people, etc.

Greenfield goes on to say that smart cities are an ideology based on scientism and positivism, which were dominant during the 19th and 20th Centuries. Siemens said it best: "Several decades from now cities will have countless autonomous, intelligently functioning IT systems that will have perfect knowledge of users' habits and energy consumption, and provide optimum service…The goal of such a city is to optimally regulate and control resources by means of autonomous IT systems" [GRE 13].

We have returned to the logical positivism of the early 19th Century which seemed to believe that the world could be perfectly known and understood and that we could design perfect systems using deductive reasoning. Logical positivism relies on the principle that reality is empirically countable and that it contains a finite number of possible relations that can be coded into a technical system, with no bias or distortion. Applied to the city, it is the argument to support that there is one and only one correct universal model which is the solution to human, individual and collective needs. The technical system, through algorithms, will find the appropriate solution depending on each input and each situation. Public policy is therefore reduced to designing the information systems that rely on data sensors and algorithms to process and interpret the data, thanks to experts that would be external to the life in the city.

We can consider this way of thinking to be undesirable, in that these algorithms will have no transparency for citizens of the city. We will revisit this essential idea of the relation between smart city and democracy. But it is mostly false on an epistemology standpoint. Logical positivism and its deductive reasoning cannot achieve a real understanding of reality. It was spread by the Vienna Circle[1] during the first half of the 20th Century and was disputed by Karl Popper, who demonstrated the error of the scientific reasoning that constituted deductive logic to which reality is only admissible insofar as it corresponds to theory.

---

1 The Vienna Circle was a group of intellectuals united around Moritz Schlick and included Rudolf Carnap, Otto Neurath, Viktor Kraft, Hans Hahn and Herbert Feigl. It attracted a number of renowned scientists such as Kurt Gödel. They set themselves the objective of unifying sciences and eliminating metaphysics, the propositions of which they considered. They were inspired by concepts from Russell and Wittgenstein with an aim to formalize scientific knowledge. Logical positivists considered that only science made sense, and only things that were empirically verifiable were scientific. Their criteria for what was scientific were also a meaningful criterion. They aspired to a world where we could base ourselves on certainty and would be rid of all metaphysics that claim to hold any truth. Popper was opposed to the philosophy of the Vienna Circle, called logical positivism, logical empiricism or even neopositivism. The criticism of this philosophy was the center of Popper's first book, *Logik der Forschung* [POP 34], *The Logic of Scientific Discovery* [POP 59].

This ideology has given way to the cult of the seamless, of continuous processes and optimization. The truth is, however, that life has seams. Everything cannot function without friction, and having seams is necessary in order to maintain data confidentiality or isolate certain processes. The obsessive scientism that comes through when discussing optimization considers the design of a perfect system that would have no elasticity in the face of unpredicted scenarios. Any system that is not simply a mechanical machine with no room for an environment that generates unpredictability requires grey areas that allow for tinkering in order to manage these unpredicted scenarios. This also means that these systems should be decentralized and grant initiative to actors in the field.

Smart cities as envisioned by salesman are therefore just a machine that will only automate existing functions reconditioned by digital technology and robots. We find here the idea of the first age of cybernetics. After the creation of the first computer, an article in *Le Monde*, "La machine à gouverner" [DUB 48] – which was very well received by one of the fathers of computing, Norbert Wiener, in *Cybernetics and Society* – states:

> "We may dream of the time when the *machine à gouverner* may come to replace – whether for good or evil – the obvious current inadequacy of the brain when the latter is concerned with the customary machinery of politics".

An old Saint-Simonian dream of replacing politics with an "industrial society" managed by the rational laws of mechanics. An automation which, just like any cybernetic system, will be incapable of facing events that have not been predicted.

Cybernetics, appearing at the end of the Second World War, was a theory founded by a meeting of the greatest researchers of the time in the field of information theory, engineering and monitoring of systems, both mechanical and social. At the end of the war, the idea was to see if self-regulated systems that used information feedback loops could provide greater regularity and serenity in human decision making. Human systems could be piloted as technical systems, thanks to engineering of complexity and control. It was considered that a system could be studied as if it were a passive piece of data that could be manipulated and perfectly described by an outside observer.

In the 1970s, a second order of cybernetics began to emerge. This new wave of cybernetics considered that reality could be piloted and understood through abstract representations – models – designed by a designer who would not be independent from the model but rather would interact with it. This allows a co-development between the observer and the model which cannot claim to be a perfect representation of reality. These models are then known as *adaptive systems* which co-evolve in this relationship between the observer and the observed. The observer is part of the problem, and the scientism present in the first order of cybernetics disappears. In this new approach, the goal is not to design a perfect city, thanks to an omniscient spirit that is above the chaos, but rather a city made through imperfect construction, one that is nonethless able to evolve thanks to a modeling process that is either intentional or unintentional if the system acquires irregular behaviors. From then, the smart city is no longer a mechanical system, but rather a human system.

1.2. The smoke and mirrors of smart cities

The dominant theory defines the smart city as an addition of "smarties": *smart people, technology, governance, building, transportation, economy, etc*[2]. This is the theory of an Austrian regional planning analyst named Rudolf Giffinger[3] developed at the Technical University of Vienna and adopted by the EU. And yet, you can have very smart people working in buildings with BIM[4] on the side, with positive energy and using Web 3.0 technologies, getting around with solar-powered electric scooters, presenting an almost Kafkaesque or Orwellian picture and resulting in a perfectly stupid reality. This notion is rooted in an approach to development that is based on exogeneous growth where technology is an outside factor, which by its very existence transforms the nature of things. This is why the European Union identifies no less than 240 smart cities in Europe based on these criteria!

---

2 Very vague criteria, and thus inhabitants are considered smart "when they prove to be flexible, creative, favorable to learning throughout life, cosmopolitan, open-minded and involved in public affairs", which corresponds to the definition of the global modern man and "citizen of the world" in neo-liberal philosophy.

3 For a presentation of the model, see: http://smart-cities.eu/model.html.

4 BIM (building information modeling) is a modeling language allowing project managers and coordinators to integrate their projects into a 6D representation (3D plus time, cost and maintenance throughout time).

The truth is, *there is, to this day, no normalized definition of what a smart city is*, no more than there is any such city on Earth, other, perhaps, than Singapore, and we will see why. What we do have, as we saw earlier, are prototypes that are showcases for technologies endorsed by our largest tech companies (Cisco, IBM, Siemens, Microsoft, etc.), such as Songdo (Korea), Masdar (Abu Dhabi) and Plan IT Valley (Portugal), but which are not cities made to be lived in by real people. Similarly, there are a large number of smart-city experiments which only deploy one aspect of a smart city, since no one to this day can define what that is, but which will serve as building blocks for a future architecture of a smart city. Most of these realizations, in fact, rely little, if even at all, on technology, but rather on a way of thinking about a city and its reconfiguration as a life system. Medellín, a city in Colombia, has, over the course of 12 years, gone from being the most criminal city in the world to a livable city based on a reconsideration of the role of transportation in people's social lives and by de-partitioning the neighborhoods.

The term "smart city" is generally associated with any urban phenomenon based on a cybernetic effect, relying on information technologies where one action is corrected by a computer on the basis of a feedback loop, generating a regulatory or even a cumulative learning process. With digital convergence, these phenomena are amplified, which allows new applications, with feedback processes occurring in nanoseconds.

The basis of a smart city is therefore its digital infrastructure which improves with the appearance of new modes of interconnectivity, such as the Internet of Things, machine-to-machine communication which removes the need for human intervention and Big Data processing. In fact, technocentric approaches are nowadays dominant in research programs.

This presents certain dangers. We saw the same phenomenon with the spread of computing. Companies began developing, on a smaller scale, technocentric approaches based on "solutions". Companies were no longer selling tools, but rather "solutions", which supposed that clients had already defined their "problems". Eric Schmidt, the CEO of Google, announced during a conference in 2012: "To connect the world is to free the world. So if we get this right, then we can fix all the other problems too…" [SCH 12a]. This is the *solutionnism* that Morozov warns about. For solutionism aficionados, the definition of a problem is its technological solution, without looking at the real causes and generally discarding all past practices. In other words, it is the solution to a problem that has not been defined, where the problem is reduced to the function of the tool.

This is dangerous because companies – and worse, public services – that have given in to this way of thinking have seen themselves lose their technical expertise or failed to develop any in situations that would have required that they update their knowledge base, have become dependent on their suppliers, who were more than happy to provide. This makes going back in any way impossible: this is the case with many cities that have delegated the management of their water to water companies under the effect of an intense propaganda campaign "private is better than public", or even injunctions such as the practices of the European Union. These cities have lost a traditional expertise and, what's more, see themselves as hostages of the water companies in the face of arbitration jurisdictions that entitle them to heavy compensations, which is what happened in Barcelos in Portugal, which had to pay the company *Aguas de Barcelos* 217 million euros because effective water consumption was lower than predicted during the deal.

This begs the question as to the place and the role of the people in a city. Greenfield tells us that when companies involved with smart-city projects talk about stakeholders, they are referring to companies, public authorities, regulators, owners and a few NGOs. But residents do not seem to exist. All they see is a sum reduced to its role of producing data through a smartphone. The goal in all of this is to provide city officials with all of the means necessary to control the life of the city. The emblematic example of this is the Control Center in Rio (Figure 1.1). A similar *Cybersyn* (contraction of cybernetic and synergy) project was designed in Chile under President Salvador Allende by British cyberneticist Stafford Beer with a project aiming to provide data to the people in reaction to the "command and control" model used by Soviet socialism. It allowed Santiago to be supplied with only 200 transport trucks driven by non-striking drivers during the truck-driver strike which attempted to starve a number of cities. Stafford Beer acknowledges the contradiction of a system designed from the top down but which in its design included the final users who should be its true proprietors: nothing like the Rio project where the stakeholders are government agencies and economic institutions.

This reduction of the resident to an adjustment variable, prevalent in smart-city promoters, is spreading through the technocentric approach pushed along by this wave of smart cities. The slide shown in Figure 1.2 was presented during a science forum by the designer of the smart-city project of a large French city. It is extracted from his excellent presentation which was the design model of a great information system as would be used in a large corporation. From a technical standpoint, it is *state of the art*. Luckily, in the last slide, the designer noticed that the residents had been completely forgotten and that their behavior cannot be reduced to that of a physical artifact. A smart city will effectively be a system with all of its elements fully integrated (we will see the definition of this in Chapter 3) in a process of architectural complexity. We nowadays have available methods for integrating objects (elements of a system) into a coherent system, but only for objects with a defined range and behavior, physical objects that have behaviors that can be defined by the laws of physics. The problem is that this cannot be done for human systems.

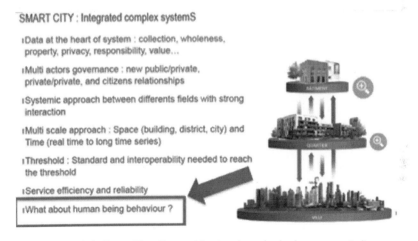

Figure 1.2. *Forgetting the residents when designing a smart city*

We see the same tendency in the Russian project Kazan smart city which reproduces Le Corbusier's functionalist diagram with very little room for the people who live there (Figure 1.3).

Figure 1.3. *The Kazan smart-city project, a reproduction of the functionalist model with very little room for the residents. For a color version of this figure, see www.iste.co.uk/rochet/cities.zip*

In all of these approaches, there is never any suggestion of the residents appropriating the data processed by these goliaths of information. The residents also have no other role than that of extras in these new "machines for living in", in the purest Le Corbusier style. As noted by Greenfield, any application of a technology rests on a hypothesis about the relation between people's behavior and said technology. In the case of a smart city, the first assumption is that urban environment has become too complex to be understood by people who must be guided and assisted via technology. The second tacit assumption is that people cannot be trusted to manage their own business: governance of the smart city must come down to the "deciders" who know how to operate the machines at their disposal. Under the seductive guise of efficiency, agility and durability, it is the old formal request for the people to submit to experts who know best. They will be given some ersatz "participation" on secondary points, as the European Union does so well, the archetype of an authoritarian system which knows how to present itself with the attractive vision of an "ecological transition" and other trendy themes[5].

At the end of the day, the debate around smart cities is nothing new: it is a return to the functional city of Le Corbusier, a city with no past, no history, a machine for living in, updated for the 21st Century with a slick marketing language and powered by powerful interests. It is the return to a notion that has already failed over 50 years of urbanism and destroys human communities. It is a voluntary and theorized ignorance of lessons from the past.

However, one could object, do these technologies not allow us to optimize certain functions, to reduce energy consumptions, to manage waste more efficiently, to improve traffic? Yes, this is all possible, but on condition that it is the end that defines the technology and not the technology defining the end, which is what we see with solutionism. Never forget one essential rule in operating complex systems: *to operate a complex system*, control its evolution and operation and not become dependent on the technologists who designed it, *it is important to master these rules of system architecture.*

We have already experienced this adventure with the deployment of computing in organizations. Tech companies already offer "solutions" to very superficially defined problems. This happened with the spread of integrated software packages (*enterprise resource planning*), extremely powerful software which are implanted into a business using state of the art comparative analysis: purchasing functions, human resources, finance and management, etc. The mistake made by many companies was to attempt to integrate the company into this software and not the other way around. This is how solutions and processes that do not correspond to the jobs and the culture of the company get hammered in.

---

5 Regarding the disappearance of politics replaced by budgetary discourse, see [ROC 11a].

It is worse, even, for those that gave in to the sirens of outsourcing. The companies and public authorities that outsourced the design of their information systems to third companies and did not develop their own technological abilities in system architecture became dependent on their providers. Many liberal countries (England, New Zealand) applied the principle of contracting out, which consists of parsing out services to private companies, which, considering the sizes of these markets, used these contracts to establish monopolies and retained the technological expertise, thus taking control of the contracted public services.

The alternative, therefore: operate the technology or be operated by it. For pessimistic authors such as Jacques Ellul[6], technology will always be able to display charms just like the sirens in Homer's Odyssey, which business managers will not be able to resist. However, as we see, while that can be the case for incompetent or lazy managers, a manager who is clear on his or her strategic objectives has a basic understanding of the dynamic of technological systems that can circumvent this pitfall and establish a healthy relationship with a provider using this approach: *system architecture.*

Is this to say, in conclusion to this chapter, that we should throw out the smart-city baby with the bathwater? Of course not, unless we were to adhere to Jacques Ellul's pessimistic vision for whom the tricks of technology will always triumph against policy. And this, in fact, is the object of this book: uncover the smoke and mirrors and propose a new approach to technology based on modeling complex systems that make technology a tool that serves a purpose, and not the other way around.

1.3. Other mirrors for other smoke: cities of the creative classes

American professor Richard Florida's reasoning was not false. The real asset for a city to attract businesses is not the plethora of tax rebates that they all offer, but the quality of its human capital. However, the argument made by Professor Florida is to first attract the human capital and then the businesses, in the idea that business will go where the talent is, which is not entirely false either.

---

6 Jacques Ellul, 1912–1994, professor of legal history and protestant theologist. His master work is *Le bluff technologique* [ELL 88].

Hence, Richard Florida's idea: cities must attract the "creative classes" to attract businesses [FLO 02] and revitalize American city centers. They represent 30% of the population and 70% of the wealth creation while covering jobs from the fields of high technology, entertainment, journalism, finance or art and craftsmanship. Richard Florida made a fortune with his ideas which were met with great success in North America. He has since started a consulting business which operates in a number of cities and spreads his theories throughout the world via conferences that bill somewhere in the vicinity of 35,000 dollars.

The city of Milwaukee, an industrial city in decline, strove to redefine its image to attract the creative classes. The results, measured on the scale of the city, are non-existent [ZIM 08], whereas the investments targeted around the city center are performed at the expense of financing equipment destined to the rest of the population. Richard Florida's approach does not work, other than the aspect of the fees spent by the mayors who have everything invested in the arrival of the "creative classes". So, why?

An in-depth study on a number of cities in Europe and North America has shown that the so-called "creative classes" are actually very sedentary and are a far cry from the myth of the globalized *smart people* who move at the whim of their desires [BOS 07]. The study showed that more than half of the sample lived in the city where they were born and educated. What makes the talent choose to move to a city? "The primary reason for their arrival is employment (51.2%) and in general the hard factors (69.9%). The soft factors only represent 10.3%, barely more than the overall population" [ECK 12]. The soft factors that are shown by the study to be truly efficient are tied to the natural environment and the atmosphere of the city, which are unlikely to be affected by public policy.

Richard Florida's reasoning is correct as far as the idea that the human capital, the social climate of a city, its culture and its history are factors of economic activity, as we will see later on when studying smart territories. But he makes the classic mistake of confusing correlation and causality. The culture of a city is a product of its industrial history and its tradition rather than a political decision and a Richard Florida-esque patchwork. A culture is the product of an endogenous emergence, resulting from history. Richard Florida's approach, on the contrary, is entirely exogenous: it would simply be a matter of importing the "creative classes". His recipe uses the rule of the "three T's": *talent, technology, tolerance. Talent*, as we have seen, is in general rather reserved and does not rush to live in the Bellevue neighborhood in Seattle – an area that is home to a portion of the "creative class" who, unlike what Florida's theory states, choose to isolate themselves from the city center – unless drawn in with high salaries by the likes of Microsoft and other tech companies that allow them to pay the sky-high rent prices that are in place there. Florida establishes a causal relation between talent and economic development. Yet, the history of economics teaches us that talent is an endogenous process which results from development and which subsequently, through a circular and cumulative relation, attracts further talent.

The focus on *technology* supposes that only high-tech companies are the basis for a territorial dynamic, when there is a dynamism within the cities that is completely ignored and which descend from a technologically obsolete past (in France, see the case of the towns of Saint-Amand-Montrond, Loos en Gohelle and Vitry-le-François, among others, which succeed the spectacular Cholet reconversion) and which have proven to be able to innovate and convert themselves from their social capital, their informal institutions and their history.

The third T, *tolerance*, is part of the current trend toward relativism. Florida even invented a *gay index* which correlates the number of homosexuals in a city with its creativity. Homosexuals supposedly fill the role of creativity indicators, like canaries in a coal mine, marking the presence of carbon monoxide. Add on top of that, a *bohemian index* to correlate the behaviors of marginal chic and creativity. For Florida, a city with no gay community and no rock bars that stay open until 3:00 has no industrial future. Here, once again, he confuses correlation and causality. That industrialization produced an evolution in morals – whether desirable or not – is evidential, but making it causality would be a fallacy.

It can seem appealing at first, and any believers in the systemic approach will no doubt be seduced by the idea that diversity is correlated with creativity. But in reality, it is actually a false diversity and a false creativity because it is based on social standards that are in appearance very rigid and thus generate an effect of increasing returns: groups attract their own, something which is in fact contained in the idea of "creative class" which only concerns about 30% of the population and who are all more or less from the same schools and programs and pay tribute to cultural values.

The failure of these theories is patent and translates to the creation of ghettos for the rich just like in Seattle and an explosion in housing prices which increase the effect of increasing returns, meaning that people find themselves located more and more with their own. Richard Florida has made a fortune; he is one of the highest paid keynote speakers in the world with a base of 35,000 dollars per conference. He now recognizes that he was wrong and continues to give 35,000 dollars to explain that his theories do nothing but reinforce social inequalities, the segregation between rich and less rich in the name of diversity, and contribute to *gentrifying*[7] major cities where the centers are being captured by a new branched elite that is evicting the *old-school* population to the periphery, but that he is not the one responsible [WAI 17].

In fact, Richard Florida and his theories only accelerated the gentrification process which affects the working class and replaces it with a new middle class who take advantage of the hike in house prices and aggravate it by rehabilitating – or more accurately using public funds to rehabilitate – old working-class neighborhoods.

The city of Seattle has done everything to conform to the policy of the three T's in coordination with the big companies within it, Microsoft and Amazon. Its urbanization plan authorized the conversion of old factories into modern offices for employees of the "creative class", who have their cycling lanes and organic gardens. All minorities have their own anti-discrimination program, and in 2012, the city won the "best city for hipsters", according to the *hipster index* which measures the number of tattoo parlors, bicycle shops, thrift stores, independent cafés open at night, craft breweries and vinyl record stores [INF 16]. Of course, it is the jobs offered by Amazon and Microsoft that attracted qualified graduates who then settle into the city center.

---

7 Gentrification is an urban phenomenon through which people with money begin appropriating a space initially occupied by people with fewer means, thus transforming the economic and social profile of the area, exclusively benefitting a higher social class. Gentry was originally used to refer to a British member of nobility and is now used with a negative connotation.

The old working-class neighborhoods are turning into fancy unaffordable buildings that offer an organic chicken farming cooperative and spas for cats and dogs. All of this is done for the "creative class", and the working class is pushed to outskirts, as the city can no longer welcome the unqualified workers (servers, cashiers, shopkeepers, etc.) that it needs: there is always a need for low-cost immigrants to deliver pizzas ordered off the Internet. Richard Florida's creative city collapses under good intentions, policies that are progressive in appearance, the "fight against discriminations", but:

> "incantations to ethnic and sexual diversity translate directly to a step back for social diversity (...) in the counties of Grant or Adams, there are no rainbow flags, no yoga clubs or vinyl record shops (...) From here the Seattle progressivism that promotes diversity but favors creative communities... that advocate for green development while the local economy depends on the intensive farming and wood-chopping, seems incongruous" [BRE 17].

As for Richard Florida, he published a new book and is still giving $35,000 conferences to explain that he was wrong and advocate for "creativity for all" and the construction of social housing, or even rent control, etc.

But what has happened to the 70% who are not "creative" according to these theories? The "useless" according to economist Pierre-Noel Giraud [GIR 15]. The eternally unemployed who live off of small jobs and welfare, who are excluded from the system and who don't even dream of entering it anymore, living on the outskirts of the "creative classes", low-cost immigrants to walk the dogs and deliver pizzas. The worst of inequalities, the one which has no future to build, no fight to fight, no horizon.

"The misery of being exploited by capitalists is nothing compared to the misery of not being exploited at all", wrote economist Joan Robinson in 1962. The old-school working class fought for a better future to improve its condition, and paved the way for healthcare systems, established labor exchanges, unions, youth movements and social tourism, and believed in a future where class solidarity would prevail. The city of the creative classes rejects this old population and its social rights and solidarities. It prefers to have legions of "useless" and hopeless people, disorganized and unable to defend themselves other than through sporadic urban riots. This is a worldwide phenomenon, described by American sociologist Saskia Sassen [SAS 12], and is the consequence of financial globalization and deregulation which centralizes the control functions to a handful of cities. In France, this is the *France périphérique* described by Christophe Guilluy [GUI 14], which is no longer under the care of central France, another global phenomenon, because it no longer needs them: the useless are enough.

Nonetheless, this does not prevent the smoke and mirrors from turning into a trap: the *"grand Paris"* project and the creation of the eponymous city are entirely based on the myth of the "creative class" and its supposed hyper-mobility. Jacques Godron [GOD 17], the President of the *Club du Grand Paris*, reapplies this idea with a number of high-ranking officials, according to a well-established French tradition to adopt the strategies that have already failed in the United States after a 10-year offset. This "Grand Paris" is investing in its *grandes écoles*, business districts, clusters, hipster culture with cat and dog spas and tattoo parlors, luxury businesses, air transport and business tourism. There is no intention of creating a housing authority which would mitigate the divide between the rich in the West and the poor in the East; that would not serve to attract

> "international business districts, CEO's, multilingual culture stars, the pioneers of R&D, press and information, international civil servants and pension funds" [GOD 15]

which do not care about inequalities, but on the contrary need the useless to proliferate and bring the creatives' dogs to the spa. All of this, the author tells us, supposes a "a subtle and accepted management model". The result, according to Christophe Guilluy, is that *"Paris is the supreme stage for a new type of capitalism. A cool capitalism that offers all of the advantages of a market economy without all of the drawbacks of a "class struggle".* In any case, as we see, a highly polluted Paris suffocates under the traffic, resulting from its dreams of being a "green city".

1.4. So what is a "smart city"?

One canonical definition of intelligence presents it as a set of processes that animate more or less complex, natural, physical systems, man-made or not, that allow them to collect data, interpret them to give them meaning, take corrective measures, learn from them and adapt to new situations. This adaptation works from the outside of the system to the inside (the system adapts to new constraints of the environment: adapts to the cold or the heat) or, conversely, from the inside out when the system adapts the environment to the requirements of its projects. The two interactions are of course tied: a smart system is in symbiosis with its environment, and there is no smart city without a smart territory.

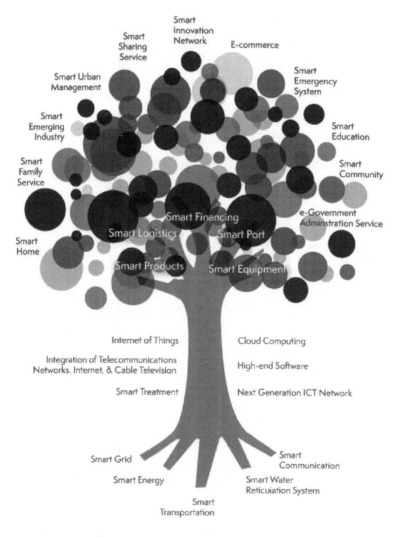

Figure 1.4. *The symbiotic vision of the smart city of Guangzhou*

A city evolves under the influence of exogenous forces, the most important of which being technology and economics. A city that is no longer able to couple its evolution with that of the economy will be doomed, as we see in the case of Russian monotowns. It will be able to evolve if it is able to *learn*, and this ability to learn will be determined by the vitality of the social fabric and the quality of formal (do they encourage this learning process?) and informal (culture, history, technological history) institutions.

The Chinese city of Guangzhou, in the Chinese strategy of appropriating Western technology, is thus defined as a smart city by its ability to integrate urban functions based on symbiosis. In a symbiotic system such as described by Isabelle Delannoy, an agricultural engineer who developed her research on the symbiotic model at the Université Polytechnique Fédérale of Lausanne [DEL 17], each function evolves by exchanging with others in order to obtain mutual benefits. The trunk of the tree integrates the physical systems that supply the sap which feeds the human systems that are the leaves. They create the energy that is sent to the roots: knowledge. This motion ensures durability. "Durable city" and "smart city" are synonymous.

SINO-SINGAPORE
GUANGZHOU KNOWLEDGE CITY
中新广州知识城

Figure 1.5. *A symbol of permanent learning, the Moebius strip*

2

The Challenges of Urban Development in the Context of the Third Industrial Revolution

Smart cities represent a market valued at US$350,000 billion over the next 30 years ($250,000 billion in infrastructure and $100,000 billion in usage), if the technological and economical model remains the same as far as rehabilitating the existing urban fabric and building new cities. In 2017, the valuation in studies on the horizon of 2020 grew to $1.209 billion [MAR 17] and even to $1.5 billion [FRO 15] for a market that was valued at $500 million in 2017. These studies add up sector infrastructure markets, including digital ones.

The current economic model of the city is not durable in the sense that it reproduces the dysfunctions present in modern cities, such as increasing emissions of pollution, waste and urban nuisances. More aggressive scenarios integrating technologies and new tools for controlling pollution emissions and improving energy efficiency estimate the volume of spending at $450 billion.

2.1. The demographic and economic challenges: toward a change in economic model

In 2008, we saw the urban population grow past 50% of the total population, including in emerging and developing countries in Latin America and Asia, with an estimated 70% growth predicted by 2030.

Urban growth is subject to a specific phenomenon of increasing returns which, according to the maths of Geoffrey West and Luis Bettencourt of the Santa Fe Institute, makes every marginal kilometer of existing infrastructure 0.85% cheaper than new infrastructure, and its resulting externalities 1.15% stronger. This is unlike a human organization – such as a company or an administration – which sees diminishing returns as its size increases. The problem is that these increasing returns affect positive externalities as well as negative ones: pollution, waste management, criminality, squalor, energy costs, etc. This growth model, born from the second industrial revolution and the "death of distance" caused by the transportation revolution during the 19th Century, is based on the consumption of fossil fuels and presents the paradox of making things easier in the short term, but non-sustainable in the medium term.

Figure 2.1. *The advantage of including positive and negative externalities when calculating costs: what appears to be an expense turns into a viable investment*

Counterintuitively, the challenge of urban development focuses more on developing countries, since the ecological footprint increases with the level of consumption (+57% every time the consumption doubles), and in small cities (population below 1 million) that increase faster.

This model knows three bottlenecks: energy consumption, pollution and social costs (stress, health, criminality, etc.) induced by a dysfunctional urban growth. Add to that and the cost of renewing infrastructures becomes considerable without providing any improvement to the current model of modern cities if they are undertaken without ever reviewing the business model.

These direct costs impact growth if they are destined to maintain the city within a constant model, when instead they can be opportunities for innovation. Considering them as management costs will lead to postponing necessary investments when, at the very least, integrating the impact of the costs of their externalities into the cost calculation makes the operation largely beneficial.

Study	Additional investment needed	GDP	Jobs and cost to businesses	Cost to families	Value of exports
	In billions	In billions	In the year 2020		In billions
Surface transportation	$846, or $94 billion a year	$897	877,000 jobs and $4,308 cost to business	$1,060 per household annual	$28 (2020 only)
Airports	$19 billion + $20 billion for NextGen, or $4 billion a year	$313	350,000 jobs and $878 cost to business	$361 billion, or $320 per household annual	$54
Marine ports and inland waterways	$16	$697	738,000 jobs and $1,838 cost to business	$872 billion, or $770 per household annual	$270
Water and Wastewater	$84 billion, or $9 billion a year	$416	669,000 jobs and $1,478 cost to business	$600 billion, or $530 per household annual	$20
Electricity	$107 or $12 billion a year	$496	529,000 jobs and $1,268 cost to business	$727 billion, or $640 per household annual	$51

Table 2.1. *Indirect cost integration highlights savings and opportunities in terms of employment and export (source: [HER 14])*

The American Association of Civil Engineers calculates that the lack of investment in water management results in a global surcharge for the economic world of $147 billion and $59 billion for households, which by 2020 will be bearing a cost of an additional $900 for water processing (Figure 2.1).

The required investment is $84 billion, which would translate to a cost reduction for businesses and protect 700,000 jobs, $541 billion in household revenue, $460 billion in GDP and $6 billion in exports (Table 2.1).

The same calculation was applied for renovating the electrical grid and the transportation network, such as ports, canals and airports. In every possible case, the return on investment as it impacts the GDP, exports, employment and household budgets is appreciable.

The current economic model of public decision is characterized by the fact that investments are postponed due to policies that enact low involvement from public power, which have been in place since the 1980s. The question of the economic model of public decision-making and its ability to integrate all externalities tied to these investments will inevitably be included in the conversation surrounding smart cities.

However, the challenges of the transition to smart cities in emerging countries are far more significant.

Urban growth in these emerging countries is very high, and the environmental impact is all the more significant as the quality of life increases. On the one hand, this development will no longer allow developed countries to externalize their polluting activities toward emerging and newly developing countries. On the other hand, from the perspective of energy consumption alone, if emerging countries were to adopt the same model as developed countries, the situation would be unsustainable; their energy consumption would quickly surpass that of developed countries within 30 years.

The experience of developed countries shows that the cost to fix a badly designed city (such as American ones, for instance, which are designed for vehicles) is far greater than the cost to build a sustainable city from the ground up. This phenomenon is well understood by system architects: a system that was not designed to be scaled must develop in successive layers which produce a "spaghetti architecture" which becomes illegible, and it becomes very complicated and costly to intervene, with unreliable results. The phenomenon is even more significant in the US where there are plenty of infrastructure stakeholders. This type of problem has driven the development of architectural methods – called "urbanization" by analogy – of information systems where the problem of spaghetti architecture is more significant because it is immaterial.

The urbanization of emerging countries is therefore a critical market both in its volume and its nature. The investment in sustainability must happen upstream during the design phase. The balance sheet of urban development in China has imitated the Western model with dramatic consequences in terms of energy consumption, waste pollution and quality of life, which has been degraded by dysfunctional cities, and illustrates the necessity of urban planning that integrates restrictions upstream.

Figure 2.2. *Spaghetti architecture within the infrastructures of New York City*

These countries still do not have the financial or, more relevantly, the technological resources to develop these integrative approaches. Western companies will therefore be solicited to ensure the transfer of technologies as emerging countries develop ambitious strategies for mastering technological abilities. Studying strategic orientation documents from Latin American countries, China and Morocco reveals the concerns of developing **integrative approaches**, rather than project by project, through ambitious public policies that highlight their necessary holistic dimensions and accentuate the coherence of sectorial policies and central and local initiatives.

The report by the OECD titled Green Growth highlights the need to dispose of a set of sophisticated tools for neutralizing the perverse effects of solutions applied unilaterally or out of context. But this set must remain legible and simple to understand and provide a frame of reference for integrating urban policy tools, rather than an exhaustive plethora of tools. **This is the challenge of developing an approach through systemic modeling**.

2.2. Geopolitical challenges: the polar shift in development in favor of the south-west and the different strategies among industrialized and emerging countries

The developmental challenges for emerging cities are those of the **industrialization of emerging countries**. Urban growth is linked to development and industrialization and has the ability to *turn the tables for powers* tied to urban development in the South and particularly in the East (Asia). McKinsey calculates that of the 600 largest cities, 380 are situated in developed countries and contributed to more than 50% of the 2007 global GDP. The 280 cities located in developing countries did not contribute more than 10% of the world's GDP. By 2025, 136 new cities will enter the top 600, and all of them will be from emerging countries: 100 of them will be in China, 13 in India and 8 in Latin America.

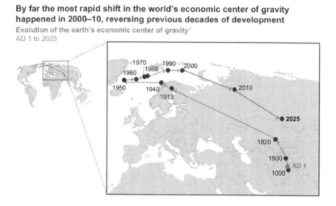

By far the most rapid shift in the world's economic center of gravity happened in 2000–10, reversing previous decades of development

Evolution of the earth's economic center of gravity¹
AD 1 to 2025

Figure 2.3. *Shift in gravity: the great return of the South. Economic center of gravity is calculated by weighting locations by GDP in three-dimensions and projected to the nearest point on the earth's surface. The surface projection of the center of gravity shifts north over the course of the century, reflecting the fact that in three-dimensional space America and Asia are not only "next" to each other, but also "across" from each other (source: McKinsey Global Institute analysis using data from Angus Maddison; University of Groningen)*

The nature of this growth will change drastically. While in 2007, 23 megacities (population of over 10 million people) produced 14% of the world's GDP, we will soon see, at the top of the 600, 230 medium-sized cities (population 150,000 to 10 million people) all in emerging countries. Contrary to the common perception, the megacities will not be the ones to drive the world's growth in the near future of 2025: 423 of the top 600 cities, all of them in emerging countries, will be middleweight cities responsible for 45% of growth.

However, this does not mean that we should only focus on these top cities. Secondary cities (population of 100,000 people or less) contribute to creating systems of cities around larger cities, which have specialized complementary roles that perform based on their connection to the urban system. This is an important point in the Latin American strategy because their cities do not receive sufficient amounts of capital or knowledge investments.

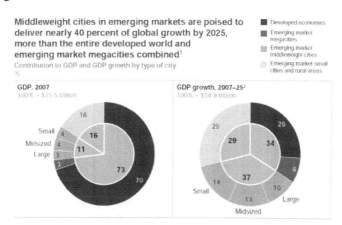

Figure 2.4. *The contribution of Western megacities to the world's growth gives way to the medium-sized cities of the emerging world*

The development of cities will not occur through a constant economic model.

In the current model for non-industrialized developing countries, urban development will happen through propagation, where shanty towns appear and are subsequently incorporated into the city (e.g. Casablanca).

This scenario relies on a system of relations between industrialized countries based on the outsourcing of activities that have negative side effects (environmental hazards, pollution, reduced working conditions) and diminishing returns to less-developed countries, thus applying the "Summers doctrine"[1]. This is a "lose-lose" scenario, in that it discourages innovation surrounding urban development in emerging countries and does not respond to the issues of environmental hazards. It highlights the necessity of **environmental accountability** which reintegrates the cost of outsourced environmental damage by importing products made in non-industrialized countries into the balance of cities in developed countries.

In the industrializing and innovative scenario, emerging countries use the fact that activities are being outsourced to organize the transfer of technologies. Rather than accentuating a quantitative accumulation of technologies, they focus on integrating them into a global approach, described as holistic, into urban planning and development in the long term. **These countries do not have the technology, but do have a political and strategic vision** of urban development. This is a classic approach to catching up that turns being behind technologically into an advantage, as theorized by Alexander Gerschenkron in his 1962[2] book. These nations can marry a traditional technology that they master and look for synergies with newly imported technologies.

---

1 Formulated in a memo by Lawrence Summers, Treasury Secretary of the Clinton administration, according to which it is more rational to outsource polluting activities toward non-industrialized countries. "I've always thought that under-populated countries in Africa are vastly UNDER-polluted, their air quality is probably vastly inefficiently low compared to Los Angeles or Mexico City [...]shouldn't the World Bank be encouraging MORE migration of the dirty industries to the LDCs [Less Developed Countries]? [...]The concern over an agent that causes a one in a million change in the odds of prostate cancer is obviously going to be much higher in a country where people survive to get prostate cancer than in a country where under 5 mortality is 200 per thousand. [...] The measurements of health costs impairing pollution depends on the foregone earnings from increased morbidity and mortality. From this point of view a given amount of health impairing pollution should be done in the country with the lowest cost, which will be the country with the lowest wages. I think the economic logic behind dumping a load of toxic waste in the lowest wage country is impeccable and we should face up to that".
2 Gerschenkron [GER 62] showed that development does not follow a linear trajectory, unlike the staged model by W.W. Rostow, but can make a delay into an advantage under the following conditions: an institutional strategy by the State which drains the physical and human capital on consumable goods and a labor-based economy, borrowing technologies from advanced countries, priority to productivity gains and activities with increasing returns rather than diminishing returns.

The Koreans, with the smart city of Songdo, marry metal-working technology in the form of their company called POSCO with digital routing imported by Cisco. They thus apply strategic innovations: the impact of one innovation does not lie in the technology itself, but rather in the synergies with older technologies. In Songdo, Cisco's expenses only make up for 2.9% of the overall budget (Cisco invested $49 billion in 2009) The rest is made up of traditional technologies such as concrete and steel made "smart" by communications' technologies.

The archetype for these long-term catch-up strategies is the Chinese strategy which is currently moving from "*made in China*" to "*innovated in China*", increasingly driven by the interior market, which clearly sets these two options: China is at a turning point in the relation between development and urbanization, the threshold of a 60% urban population. It either pursues a tendency scenario toward a non-smart urbanization, or it adopts an innovative strategy linking cities with economic, social and political development[3].

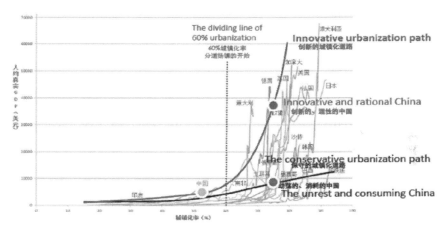

Figure 2.5. *Linking innovation and urban development: the Chinese strategy (source: professor Wu Zhiqiang)*

3 Intervention by Professor Wu Zhiqiang, Vice President of University Tongji, at a seminar on smart cities, Shanghai, October 2014.

In this industrialist holistic strategy, Western technology is acquired by partnerships that are the condition for entry into the Chinese market, or even through "honeypot" strategies destined to attract these industries in clusters. Thus, inviting the French to build model smart cities in Chengdu, Wuhan and Shenyang allowed the Chinese to attract all of France's expertise onto a delineated geographic perimeter.

The strategies of industrialized countries are centered around sector-specific markets that correspond with their technological offerings. Therefore, while an English research paper [DEP 13] highlights the need to develop – indiscriminately, presumably – global offers, it is structured around five vertical sectors of British offerings: water, transportation, waste, energy and housing. The French strategy, developed by the previous Minister for Foreign Trade, while claiming to attempt to develop a global offer around "living well in the city", has remained an additive to the offers of French businesses. The report from the *Commissariat Général au Développement Durable*[4] even moved backwards on these new approaches by attempting to organize French offerings into activity sectors, before realizing how little sense such an approach would make since "smart cities lead industrials to adopt an open approach" [CGD 12].

Conversely, **the strategies of emerging countries focus on integration** which relies on politico-institutional strategies and not just technologies. Emerging countries formulate their urban strategy in terms of long-term development, not just in terms of commercial results as is so often the case in industrialized countries. The Chinese report defines its political objective to be to build livable cities that can grow sustainably in accordance with the principles of an ecological civilization. Thus, China has gone from a development-centric strategy that favors functional urbanism, known as "copy and paste urbanism", to an integrationist urbanism. The law surrounding urban and rural development, passed in 2008, marks a significant turning point. It confirms the importance of social and environmental matters in the face of economic matters. Cities are no longer considered part of a quantitative extending dynamic, but as part of a renewable qualitative ideology. The key notion here is that of "beauty" and harmony, aiming to reconcile all dimensions of our cities [DOU 15].

---

4 Department of the Commissioner General for Sustainable Development.

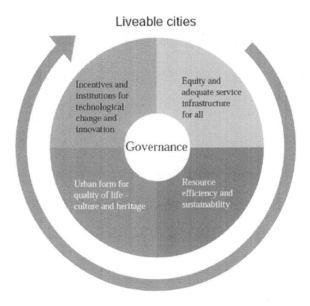

Figure 2.6. *The Chinese path to livable cities*
(source: China Human Development Report 2013 [UND 13])

Figure 2.6 represents **China's strategy**, which balances five dimensions:

– **Equity**: in the ancient philosophy of yin and yang, imbalance is more dangerous than rarity. In addition, the out-of-control growth of the past few decades has made China one of the most unequal countries in the world with a Gini coefficient in the order of 0.6.

– **Efficiency**: with the blind expansion in the past decades, China has seen prices skyrocket along with wasted resources. The mistakes from China's urban policies are attributed to an error in the perception of the role played by the government in urban development. Here, the government should be seen as a designer rather than a monitor; a hierarchy that favors size above all else, and an erroneous notion that large cities are always the best cities. The responsibility is thus placed on the necessary leadership to integrate stakeholder contributions into a shared strategic vision of urban development.

– **Sustainability**: this looks at technological and human objectives.

- Technological: the cost in energy and the increasing demand for resources, the immaturity of technologies, the adjustment in industrial structure and the context.

- Human: residents must be able to live where they work, thus development must focus on residents.

– **Innovation**: in this case, innovation correlates with the ability to integrate cultural heritage rather than copying European architecture for tourism and business. The uniformization of cities indicates a lack of creativity and innovation.

– **Security**: whether it be economic, social, environmental or dietary, security must move past the conversation about citizens' rights. This strategy focuses on education and the development of a social capital and civic spirit.

This multidimensional strategy is coherent with the state-of-the-art economics of innovation: material capital is mobile and can therefore be copied, while immaterial effects (knowledge, expertise, social capital) are rooted to a territory and are not highly mobile. Thus, immaterial effects must be reproduced endogenously by learning from the historical specificities of the social capital of the territory. Abilities are idiosyncratic in nature, meaning they belong to a context or an organization and are difficult to employ in another form. While a technology can be copied, an ability cannot. The latter must be recreated through a long learning process endogenous to the hosting country and territory. It depends on a technological culture, which in turn is dependent on social capital.

This, in fact, is the etymological meaning of the word *techno-logy*, as historians in economic development are rediscovering and as the thinkers of Western Enlightenment philosophy, Francis Bacon, Giambattista Vico and Blaise Pascal, understood it. The term is composed of *techné*, technique, the mechanical which works off the same principle as an automation, and *logos*, tacit and explicit knowledge (Figure 2.7). Recent works on the history of economics, in particular, those by Professor Joel Mokyr at Northwestern University [MOK 02], highlight the confusion – which gradually infected Western thinking – between technique and technology. This confusion leads us to forget the immaterial and cultural aspect at the heart of the true competitive advantage of businesses and nations, which has been the driving force behind previous industrial revolutions.

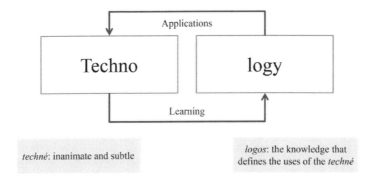

Figure 2.7. *Technology is essentially just knowledge*

Emerging countries have a strategy based on integrating existing technologies they can acquire from industrialized countries, while the former have strategies based on exportation. On the one hand, the medium-term integrative strategies dictate the demand; on the other, the additive short-term strategies of industrialized countries dictate the supply. A common frame of reference based on the development of systemic modeling would rebalance this probable leadership inversion in favor of emerging countries.

2.3. Energy transfer: the fossil fuel curse is not about to disappear

Two recent works, Carbon Democracy by Timothy Mitchell [MIT 11] and Or Noir by Matthieu Auzaneau [AUZ 15], highlight how much fossil fuels have shaped our social and political systems. The energy behind the first industrial revolution was coal, which caused a dissociation between areas of industrial production and rich housing communities fleeing Coketown. However, as Timothy Mitchell explains, coal production was centralized into areas that concentrated working-class laborers and was shipped via specific and localized canals, which also required laborers. This allowed the working class to promote workers' rights, improving their conditions beginning with their housing and health, and establishing unions, or labor exchanges, which contributed to a lost ecosystem of life that disappeared with the exodus to the city.

With the transition to oil, an energy that is easy to transport, production areas were spread outside of working class living areas, and things began to change. Keep in mind that the young revolutionary Joseph Stalin was an oil worker in Baku, where he pushed for revolutionary strikes. But the power of oil would destroy this labor power. On top of this, oil shapes global geopolitics: the great oil companies such as a Standard Oil organize oil shortages in order to drive up the prices and maintain control over the production points. The problems in the Middle East today are, for the most part, a result of borders drawn by Western powers (Britain, United States, France) according to the locations of oil-rich areas in Iraq and Syria, which gave birth to nations that do not correspond to their history.

The power of oil shaped modern cities in accordance with their needs. Shortly thereafter, oil companies, Renault in France, and General Motors in the United States, torpedoed electric tramway systems replacing them with buses. Paris' streetcar network was the largest in the world and connected the city to its suburbs. It was done away with between 1930 and 1932 to make way for Renault buses. In 1935, the United States Congress forbade energy companies from owning streetcar holdings. General Motors then bought these holdings and deliberately let the infrastructures deteriorate. Two years later, GM began dismantling the streetcar networks throughout the major American cities. GM was reprimanded in 1949 along with Firestone and Standard Oil, but the damage was done [JAR 17].

Leaving the oil era behind would therefore be a blessing, but economic history teaches us that such a change only happens if it is cost effective. In addition, as we saw in the Introduction, this is gradually becoming the case, though the death of petrol is not imminent. For the International Energy Agency (IAE), the energy market will continue to grow until 2040: oil consumption will go from 90 million barrels a day in 2016 to 121 million barrels a day in 2040. Oil is not done shaping global geopolitics – something Jean-Michel Valantin points out [VAL 17] – what with China's growing oil needs to ensure its transition out of coal, which is the source of the unlivable pollution in its cities. Oil and gas will structure a new age of geopolitics around the New Silk Road, the Chinese strategy for securing its energy provisions, relying on the Russian Arctic, via a route that will go from Iceland to the Middle East, and will be twice the size of the ancient Silk Road that crossed Central Asia. Nonetheless, the end of the oil economy is nigh. The classic oil deposits have reached *peak oil*, even though that deadline keeps moving further back with the growing presence of unconventional hydrocarbons.

Even with the new impulse given by the use of the Russian Arctic, oil's diminishing returns are appearing. The energy return on investment (ERI) [HAL 17] was originally excellent and was the driving factor behind the second industrial revolution. But from an ERI of 60 to 1 (1 barrel consumed to produce 60), it is down to 10 to 1, whereas that of green energies remains far below, reaching 1 to 1 for biofuels. Hall estimates that the required ERI to power an industrial society is somewhere between 10 to 15. This means we will not only need to change the nature of the energy we consume, but, supposing that renewable energies are able to substitute fossil fuels, *the way that we consume energy* (i.e. our living systems) will have to change, starting with the urban systems.

Let's not kid ourselves about sustainable energies: in an invigorating book [PRU 17], professor Rémy Prud'homme shows that the maturity and deployment of renewable energies for the production of electricity are not anywhere near the levels portrayed by certain politicians and industry leaders. Their production capacity and returns are effectively low, and there is a lot of misinformation in circulation. Public financing can lead to deployment of technologies that have not yet reached technological maturity. This is the case for Denmark, an exception that does not confirm the rule. Comparing Danish production and consumption, argues Remy Prud'homme, can make one dream of a potential for electric self-sufficiency based on harnessing the energy of the sun and wind. However, the hours during which Denmark consumes are generally not the ones during which it produces. In the absence of a vast capacity for electrical storage, the country can only function through its integration into a larger grid that includes Sweden and Norway (and their hydraulic and nuclear electricity). Not to mention that Denmark produces electricity that no one wants, and it is forced to pay to get rid of it. Renewable electricity is still, to this day, hindered by the inability to store it. It is therefore not mature.

Renewable energies do not free us from the geopolitical agendas of their promoters, similar to the oil era. China maintains a quasi-monopoly on rare earth minerals necessary to the digital industry. There will be geopolitics driven by the digital economy, the same way that geopolitics is currently driven by oil. In the name of the fight against climate change, emerging countries are being banned from building energy farms using fossil fuels. Parts of Africa are in dire need of electricity, but they are not expected to create fossil fuel plants using a readily accessible technology. This is a typical case of a "kicking away the ladder" strategy similar to the one that developed countries applied against other nations after the first industrial revolution[5].

For Development Economics Historian Erik Reinert, we have entered a sixth development cycle[6] based on "green technology" for which the industry is now entering a phase of increasing returns [REI 15]. Industry interests would therefore become compatible with a respect for the planet's ecological limitations, which is good news, because in the real world – specifically in the capitalist world – things do not change for good, but because it becomes more cost effective. For Australian management professor John Mathews [MAT 13], this is a "Schumpeter" socioeconomical paradigm shift as identified by Carlota Perez, which would follow the fifth paradigm shift based on information technologies [ROC 15b]. A change in paradigm means that we are entering a continuous learning cycle and a cost reduction cycle. One such cycle occurs in two ways: through process innovation (or learning curve) and by applying these processes to increasing production volumes. Both phenomena are inseparable. Economist Nicholas Kaldor characterized this process as a chain reaction: the more costs drop, the higher the returns increase, and the more incentive there is to develop this new industry.

In addition, as we progress along the learning curve by solving occurring problems, polluted countries – India and China – are in the best positions with their green growth to take leadership in this new and growing industry, while the Western world runs the risk of being trapped by fossil fuels, and the dominant industries benefit from vested interests, allowing them to lobby intensely in favor of the status quo (generally through over-employment blackmail).

The East's green development strategy rests on the hypothesis that renewable energies are reaching maturity. However, the real technological break will be an innovation in energy storage. Without that, renewable energies remain intermittent and dependent on their pairing with gas and oil. During the second industrial revolution, electricity was not an improvement upon the candle, but a radical split. This is not the case with the wind

---

5 Kicking away the ladder has been described by Friedrich List in his 1846 book [LIS 46]: England prospered thanks to protectionism and reached the "top of the ladder" and then attempted to prevent its competitors from accessing the ladder in the name of free trade. See [ROC 14].
6 For the history of development cycles, see [REI 08].

turbine, which is just an improved fan, an incremental improvement combined with an improved turbine [PRU 17]. This industry is not managed as an innovative industry: it mostly depends on large companies and benefits from public financing. In France, there are no French companies. The only two were sold: Alstom was sold to General Electric and Areva sold its subsidiary to a Spanish conglomerate, which was subsequently bought by Siemens. Thus, the progression along the learning curve does not benefit France's economy. Since Schumpeter, we know that an industrial revolution is driven by entrepreneurs who take innovative, industrial and financial risks. There are no great entrepreneurs in renewable energies that are over-financed with public money for the benefit of large international industrial corporations. Because of this, we are witnessing cities finance the installation of electric automotive charging stations: did the second industrial revolution have public funding financing gas pumps? Contradictorily, modern politics make renewables – which are currently limited to wind farming and solar panels, omitting nuclear, biomass and many others – a vested interest. If these industries require support from nascent industries [ROC 14], it is for the purpose of building a new market, which cannot be on the agenda.

2.4. The six breakthroughs in urban development based on smart cities

As we've seen, smart cities will not appear from the addition of technologies, no matter how effective. Nor will their development be a result of market forces alone. It will be a global change, a breakthrough. The digital economy of the third industrial revolution – now known as the *i*conomy[7] – allows us to establish multiple connections between residents and objects and reinvent business models. It isn't technology that makes a city smart, but its ability to be a city in the classic sense: with a diversity of activities, an ability to evolve naturally – known as organic growth – from its own set of operating rules, with no centralized planning, through an active civic life.

Approaching a city as a life system highlights **six disruptions, six great challenges** that affect all aspects of our social, economic, political and geopolitical lives.

---

7 *i*conomy: French portmanteau of *informatique* (digital) and *économie* (economy).

A geostrategic break will occur because emerging countries will be the ones to experience the highest demographic and urban growth. Added to this are geopolitical breaks linked with climate change. The increase in forest fires is saturating the rescue services which can no longer cooperate. The opening of the Russian Arctic to travel will save them from crossing Africa through the Suez Canal and the Malacca strait and open up possibilities giving birth to an ambitious plan for Russia to urbanize the Arctic. All of these elements of thought and these new contexts highlight the notion of cities as a whole, as life systems that integrate work, housing, social and civic life. Thus, the Casablanca smart city project aims to remedy the out-of-control growth of the city – 300 hectares every year – and its monstrous pollution. Meanwhile, industrialized countries have industrial offers regarding urban subsystems (transportation, energy, water, housing, infrastructure, environment, etc.) and are not yet ready to develop a global offer that would have to be more than the sum of all of these subsystems. The South has the markets, the North has the technologies, but technologies that are not currently integrated into a systemic global model of the city. Therefore, the challenge is for the South to develop the methodologies (soft), which will help them integrate the material technologies (hard).

This requires a **scientific breakthrough**, because a city is more than the sum of its buildings and more than an aggregate of its cutting-edge technologies. The city is a complex ecosystem, the rules of which are still beyond us. This includes emerging countries such as China that are working to highlight this integration and modeling effort of the city as a *life system* governed by a harmony among the elements, a principle at the heart of some Chinese philosophy. Whoever masters the ecosystem of the city will *de facto* master the underlying technologies, define the demand and the supply for smart-city construction, and will define the standards in a field that is still largely unknown despite such a ubiquitous point of focus. If we look at the expansion of Singapore [ROC 17a], we can see that absorbing hard technologies is actually relatively easy, and as soon as a country has understood that the keys to success are in intellectual investment of soft technologies and social capital, the student overtakes the master in only a matter of decades.

Managerial disruption will be necessary because this project will require an in-depth transformation of business models for governments and businesses. Businesses – many of which have already started – must collaborate along the principle of "coopetition" to develop global offerings and integrate positive and negative externalities (unchecked induced effects) when calculating the return on investment. In the 1920s, British economist Arthur Cecil Pigou suggested integrating the cost of externalities (pollution, increasing transportation costs due to globalization, waste management, etc.) when calculating the cost of investments. A city can be green in appearance, but one must take into account in its economic and ecologic balance its pollution and the social costs of products that are being manufactured overseas in low-salary factories. The pollution generated by the Chinese industry mainly comes from the demand for low-cost products from the Western world. When the city of Séné, in Brittany, buys its granite in China to save money, the resulting pollution and social costs in China must be considered, along with the transportation and its impact on the environment and the loss of jobs in Brittany.

A **split in public policies** will occur because public authorities must be capable of thinking "city" and developing new abilities in system architecture, which implies a profound evolution of administrative organization which must operate transversally as it is impossible to think in terms of complex systems with an administration compartmentalized into silos. Thinking about a city also means thinking about the coherence of the social fabric that makes up a city: its life system and its relation to its suburbs. The impact of globalization is noxious, in that it causes a metropolization of activities with a high economic potential and a high decisional content. In sociological terms, this translates to an over-representation of high executives appropriating housing in the once working-class areas and the development of suburbs into areas for under-qualified immigrant labor.[8] Metropolization causes a double phenomenon of social decomposition: within its urban fabric, which divides into two extreme poles, and the city and its suburbs, which become unindustrialized. If the city is rich and competitive, there is no invisible hand to harmoniously distribute this wealth: urban violence in suburbs and popular revolts of surrounding cities have become phenomena common in all advanced capitalist countries.

A **social and technological split** will occur because the digital economy – *i*conomics – is a new field which cannot be left to the big players such as GAFAM (Facebook, Apple, Microsoft, Google, Amazon), the market

---

8 The case of Paris is, in this case, emblematic. See the works by Anne Clerval on the gentrification of Paris [CLE 16].

capitalization is now equivalent to France's GDP. In *i*conomics, virtually everything can be connected to everything else – in particular with the Internet of Things – and create an unchecked complexity. It is important to define what must remain human and what can be incorporated into a technical system. For instance, a car can brake automatically if it is too close to another car. This increases safety, but the system must be more than 100% reliable in practice since it has to be redundant. Furthermore, cars equipped with effective systems will encounter vehicles that are not equipped with this technology. Therefore, we must navigate between passive and active safety, perform studies in ergonomics, etc. To design this, competing companies must cooperate with one another and with specialists in social sciences, which is still not present in today's business models. Another vast worksite is that of Big Data, which allows businesses to establish correlations helpful for understanding human behavior or predicting events. However, this can be detrimental to data confidentiality and develop overly intrusive control systems. This is also a split with the current urban development model, which creates gaps between production facilities and consumption locations. Polluting activities have been pushed outwards toward poor countries and the outskirts of cities with working class neighborhoods. This policy was adopted at the end of the 19th Century and worsened throughout the 20th Century along with the impossibility of finding a solution to the problem of pollution[9]. This approach pushed the poor to the outskirts of cities. The discourse surrounding sustainable cities, green cities and inclusive cities is just a social lie if the environmental costs of manufacturing countries and negative externalities such as traffic and pollution being moved to the outskirts are not reintegrated.

A **political split** is necessary because smart cities can also become the hell imagined by Jeremy Bentham in the early 19th Century with his panopticon – a society of generalized surveillance – if we follow a utilitarian approach guided only by the optimization of costs and the power of technology, rather than a city for its people where living is good. Throughout the history of urban development, Lewis Mumford shows us that the forces of the markets have been the drivers for urban degeneration by focusing solely on the pursuit of profit by promoters at the expense of the equilibrium of the city. Tall towers made fortunes for elevator companies and optimized the housing prices by concentrating housing and creating congested city

---

9 See the beautiful, engaging and unique book on this subject by Francois Jarrige and Thomas Le Roux [JAR 17].

centers, where getting around with a car is slower than a horse-drawn carriage and resulted in forced exoduses to dysfunctional city suburbs. We will have to reinvent the use of public construction around the notion of smart city as designed as an ecosystem. At the core of this complexity, residents will have to reacquire power in order to not be consumed by an Orwellian hell, which may bring the spotlight back on direct democratic practices and political control, which developed at the beginning of urban civilization, and will now be augmented by the power of digital.

To conclude, **smart cities are more of a political project rather than a technical vision** of the future of society and its values.

3

What Makes a City Smart?

The word "smart" is often associated with technological systems. Any system that self-regulates on the basis of a retroactive phenomenon is qualified as smart, similar to a thermostat. Intelligence is defined as the ability to modify one's behavior according to the result following an action. This regulation occurs empirically following the principle of *induction*, meaning that we *infer similarity from similarity*. This is the white swan principle: after noting that N swans are white, I infer that all swans are white. This principle will lead the system to make "more of the same", for example, a thermostat undertaking certain actions to attain the desired temperature. However, the system can enrich its operation by integrating theoretical resources – which do not come from empirical experience – which can lead to another way of doing something, in this case, because the digital introduces another possibility of doing things and regulating the urban system. This is the principle of *deduction*, which goes from a theory to practice.

The *smart cities* movement introduces new theories that modify traditional regulations of urban operation, based on the fact that the empirical regulation system only leads to reproducing unsatisfactory situations. Innovation in that case, if there is any, is entirely *exogenous*, meaning that it comes from outside of the urban system. This is the whole point, from a marketing strategy perspective, of attaching an ideological aspect to a tool offered to a socio-economic stakeholder who is noticing that empirical solutions no longer work.

The problem with this approach is that it only produces automatic reactions. We are in a case of simple regulation: with the arrival of digital technology, we introduce new regulatory tools, but they only tend to maintain the system in homeostasis. The conversation surrounding smart cities only sees the city develop through the promise of a technological evolution that will always provide more possibilities of a mythical *new age*, which is dependent on technology manufacturers. For this system to be truly smart, it needs the ability to learn. In addition, learning is the ability to question one's own starting hypotheses, *infer difference from similarity*, which in epistemology is known as *abduction*, or, to reuse Karl Popper's expression made popular by Nassim Nicholas Taleb, the theory of the black swan: seeing that 99 swans are white does not mean we should infer that the 100th is white as well, which is effectively what happened when we discovered black swans in Australia.

The principle of intelligence innovation evolution supposes a give and take between technology and the empirical, while accounting for history that structures our *endogenous* way of learning – what is known as path dependency (the more we learn, the more we know how to learn and the more we subscribe to a way of learning and accumulate social and cultural capital). The discourse surrounding smart cities completely ignores this endogenous ability to evolve which has been at the core of intelligent cities in the past.

3.1. Lessons from medieval cities

Medieval cities were intelligent in that they constituted coherent communities that adapted to the functions of the city and its relations to its outskirts. These cities did not have architects in the modern sense of the word; there were no urban planning laws, no building permits. These cities grew organically. Through endogenous growth, they developed from an analysis of the need to establish urban functions and a community based on the values of its residents, depending on economic activity, religion and the protection of their rights and liberties acquired from their feudal masters.

For Lewis Mumford

> "Organic planning does not begin with a preconceived goal; it moves from need to need, from opportunity to opportunity, in a series of adaptations that themselves become increasingly coherent and purposeful, so that they generate a complex final design, hardly less unified than a pre-formed geometric pattern (…). Though the last stage in such a process is not clearly present at the beginning, as it is in a more rational, non-historic order, this does not mean that rational considerations and deliberate forethought have not governed every feature of the plan, or that a deliberately unified and integrated design may not result" [MUM 11].

To say these cities had no architects in the modern sense does not mean they had no detailed plans, because there were often plans, but they were *generic plans*, even for new cities such as the *bastides*[1], which appeared to result from geometrical plans when in fact the urban plan "*is only the culmination of multiple trials and the fruit of further reconfigurations*" [BOU 03]. Cases of cities from regular plans were rare, like Montauban in 1144. Medieval expert Jacques Heers states "*Uniformity, when it occurs, is simply a matter of a need for practicality, of benefiting from past experiences, not an intellectual attitude, of a petition of principles which would claim to return to ancient criteria or submit to its 'modules'*" [HEE 90].

3.1.1. *Architect-less cities?*

These cities were built without architects, but residents had a shared vision of what beauty is, which meant that each of them was responsible for integrating their lot into an overall harmonious system. There were no building permits because no one would have ever dreamt of building something ugly in a harmonious balance. As Mumford explains, "*The consensus surrounding the goals of urban life was so entrenched that any variation would only serve to reinforce the model*". This highlights the contrast between baroque formalism – an illusion of order following the Middle Ages – and the asymmetries and irregularities of the cities of the

---

1 French fortified cities.

Middle Ages, which *"take into account the most subtlety thought-out necessity for practical order and aesthetic imperatives"*.

It was the Italian, French, and Hanseatic merchant towns, as well as Novgorod the Great (*Veliki Novgorod*) and Pskov in Russia, that had certain liberties based on direct democracy [SIN 11]. Until the sacking and subjection of Novgorod in 1478 by Tsar Ivan III, the city was ruled by a relatively pure form of the popular Republic. We see this today in the *landsgemeinde* of Swiss-German regions; the *veche* (вече), where anyone who rung the bell could call an assembly to deliberate on a subject. Princes who called the *veche* were bound by convention to the city and responsible for the people who could end their reign, which is what happened in 1136 when the Novgorodians chased out their prince. A sense of the common good and a global aesthetic linked to democratic deliberation meant that problems stemming from urban medieval organization (guilds, traffic, interfaces between cities and their outskirts, religious life and civic life) were easily solved. "Veche *is certainly the most essential notion in Russian culture"*, explains Olga Sevatyanova in a wonderful book on Novgorod [FRI 15]. All decisions were made through a consensus, and this became the reference for the liberal reforms of the 19th Century, after the abolition of serfdom in 1861 and *zemstvos* were established to autonomously manage lands at a local level.

Figure 3.1. *The* Veche *in Pskov*

A city was a learning experience, a permanent collective process for solving problems that contributed to a shared cultural and methodological baggage. This system was not a projection of an ideal city – something we will find in many later works from Thomas More's *Utopia,* to the garden cities of Ebenezer Howard and the new technological utopia of *smart cities* – but of the profound conscience that a city was a system in constant imbalance, perpetually under threat from the struggle between the many and the few and – at times when the few subjugated the many – by fratricidal struggles of the powerful against one another.

Cities are a space for conflict resolution, whether they be social or political conflicts, or violence endogenous to the urban fabric, or the violence imported by the insecurity of the countryside. This is how a civic religion develops, that of the common good; a middle ground between ancient virtue and the expectancies of urban government, which the Christian Aristotelian Marsilius of Padua synthesized in his thesis *De Defensor Pacis*, and to which Ambroggio Lorenzetti makes an allegorical reference in his mural *Allegory of Good Government* that decorates the City Hall in Siena (Figure 3.2). The link between the institutional organization of the struggle between classes and the pursuit of common good is at the core of Machiavelli's famous 16th Century book.

As time went on, this civic religion gave us the *Palazzo municipale* and its *Piazza civile,* which is one of the rare buildings to be subjected to a detailed plan as the physical incarnation of the *political architecture* of the city.

Without realizing it, this systemic dynamic dealt with one of the most arduous problems we face today when modeling cities as complex systems: **The limits of a city and its interaction with the surrounding countryside.** These limits were once represented by the walls around a city, initially built for security purposes, but which also had an essential political and functional role. These walls created a sense of community and managed the interactions between a city's economic activities and those of its surrounding areas. This is where German economist Johann Heinrich von Thünen came up with his early 19th Century location theory, which explains that economic activities such as extensive agriculture and industry are distributed concentrically in circles. Activities that provided increasing returns were at the center, surrounded by activities with more and more diminishing returns the further out of the city you go.

The desirability of an area can therefore be seen as a system of interdependencies structured by synergies created by the city center. Von Thünen's industrial location theory [THÜ 42] accounted for the desire of Renaissance economists to build a general system of interdependencies for economic activities structured around cities, a vision that modern economics would abandon in favor of Ricardo's theories[2]. A monotown with a single activity creates very few synergies and therefore causes the territory to lose its appeal.

Figure 3.2. *The effects of a good government, from a series of murals by Ambroggio Lorenzetti. It illustrates the rotation of offices of political responsibility, participation in civic activity, synergy between commercial and artisanal activities and the interface between city and countryside*

---

2 Schumpeter placed von Thünen far higher than Ricardo and his theories of comparative advantages, which ignored interdependencies: *"the complete view of universal interdependence of all elements of the economic system that haunted the spirit of Thünen, probably never cost Ricardo an hour's sleep"* [SCH 87].

3.1.2. *How do cities become unintelligent?*

Looking at medieval cities also shows us why such a model failed. Mumford explains that *"the walls created a sense of exclusive insularity which, in the end, proved to be fatal"*. The dynamic of a system is its ability to redefine its boundaries when the environment changes. If medieval cities provided a good example of a network of medium cities each representing a "Thünen zone", they were isolated by poor roads and insecurity. With the revolution of transportation – the "death of distance" – this urban dynamic disappeared in favor of monofunctional cities.

One conjunctural element of great magnitude was to hit this urban dynamic: the bubonic plague of 1348 which wiped out a third of Europe's population and roughly half of the population of the cities. As the epidemic affected groups organized around regular contact, communal institutions were hit hard. The clergy and monastic orders were particularly affected, and they represented the backbone of intellectual development and were harboring the blossoming bud of Renaissance political thinking. What followed was superstition and a relationship with power bereft of principles.

The Great Plague contributed to two parallel political developments which shaped the urban dynamic of cities: the rise of absolutism saw cities as a symbol of power, favoring baroque centralized planning to organic planning, as was the case in Saint Petersburg, built by modernist Tsar Peter the Great. A beautiful city that integrated foreign contributions to Russian culture, Saint Petersburg was built by thousands of serfs, many of whom died in the awful working conditions. The city of Yekaterinburg in the Ural is the exact opposite of Veliki Novgorod, which grew organically. It was founded in 1723 and began as a giant factory. Its founder, Vasily Tatischev, associated this urban approach with a political ideal: autocracy. The apparent mess of an organic city disappears in favor of geometric rigor, a city is no longer an expression of a system of life, of bottom-up organic growth, but of a top-down authoritarian order that represents the power of its prince.

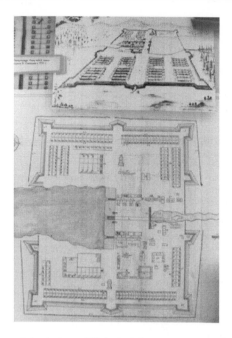

Figure 3.3. *The original plan of Yekaterinburg as a monofunctional factory city (photo by the author, Museum of the city of Yekaterinburg)*

The old regime of collective liberties then moved towards the individual liberties of capitalism, which contributed to the loss of a vision that considered a city as a cohesive whole in favor of the optimization of a single parameter – such as land value – towards a singular objective: short-term financial profit.

The city loses its intelligence first through the submission of its development and its plan to the visions of political power, which expects a strict order; tidy plans that split from the apparent disorder of medieval cities that represented a human experience of the city. *"Life becomes an instrument of order"*, as Lewis Mumford puts it. The "death of distance" means that cities can finally scale the walls they had built. Cities begin to develop beyond their walls, losing their coherence in the process.

With the development of industry starting in the early 19th Century, they lose their coherence: *"From then on, construction works depended on the*

initiatives of bankers, industrialists or inventors of new technologies"
explains Lewis Mumford. The sense of the common good disappears with
the affirmation of the myth of individual liberties: *"anyone and everyone
was looking to become a despot in his own kingdom"* [MUM 11]. There have
been no improvements to urban life with industrialization. On the contrary,
any study concerning the quality of life in society – which, contrary to a
certain popular misconception, was a very important factor for classic
economists such as Adam Smith – disappears in favor of a frantic pursuit of
progress, with little to no ethical considerations. It is the birth of Coketown,
a representation of Manchester from Charles Dickens' book *Hard Times*
(1854), which expresses the full horror of a stunted city, sacrificed in the
sole name of industry, polluted and dirty. *"Until 1838, neither Manchester
nor Birmingham even functioned politically as incorporated boroughs: they
were man-heaps, machine-warrens, not organs of human association"*.

While medieval cities were filled with Renaissance humanism and
political philosophy and articulated around a social and political life, making
them places of emancipation and liberty – as goes the German proverb,
"city air makes you free" – the Coketown era is that of the materialism
predominant in Western politics, in which only increasing utility
can improve peoples' lives. The middle class that owned the factories
was convinced of its righteousness thanks to liberal theories
(Manchesterism[3]) and the apology of the industrial city, which appears as
modern and clean in comparison to ancient artisanal activities – like
tanneries – generating stench and pollution. It was the era of Saint-Simon,
who saw in the industry the means for humanity's transformation.
The English chemist Andrew Ure [URE 36], in a book titled
The Philosophy of Manufactures, set the tone: *"Such is the factory system
(...) which promises, in its future growth, to become the great minister of
civilization to the terraqueous globe"*. He explains that the great chimneys
are a step forward from the smaller workshops, breweries and foundries of
the artisanal production model.

---

3 Liberal doctrine developed by the British industrial class that favors free-trade and low
government involvement.

Figure 3.4. *Photo of Manchester, illustration of Coketown for Charles Dickens'* Hard Times

3.2. A city is a system of life

Cities are not material artifacts; they are first and foremost complex social systems. Thanks to digital technology, the need for human interaction can be greatly facilitated, but it cannot define the finality of life within a city. What is the point of human communication when crammed into a transportation system that sterilizes all communication and where people wait to get home so they can communicate with their virtual "friends" via social networks?

Thus, the need for an approach to innovation that does not stem from technology but rather from humans is that of *living labs* – living ecosystems that involve all stakeholders of a city and all scientific fields both "soft" (social sciences) and "hard". The *living lab* must represent the whole diversity of the urban ecosystem and produce scenarios and strategies.

In the current state of research, both camps – technocentric and citizen-centric – do not converge. "Fireball" [SCH 12b] is a European research program which notes three important gaps that must be filled: the capacity, of both companies and citizens, to develop web-based solutions; the gap in creativity between the core of web-based technologies and their ability to produce useful applications; and an entrepreneurial gap between these applications and their translation into innovative services. We can develop an understanding of the problems posed by these interactions and understand their principles through the *living lab* approach, pilot projects paired with research projects and heavy involvement from users.

Luis Bettencourt [BET 13a, BET 13b], a systems expert at the Santa Fe Institute, insists that a city is **a complex adaptive system**, or, more specifically, a **system of systems**[4]. An adaptive system can only be defined in detail before the fact according to the principles of detailed engineering and first order. The problems that a city will encounter or that can arise from designing the perfect city can only be identified in a top-down fashion, something that became apparent in the 20th Century in England and the United States with Ebenezer Howard's garden cities, as well as Le Corbusier in France and in Soviet architecture.

Bettencourt insists on the importance of resisting the temptation to plan everything in great detail. In the tradition of biologists such as Patrick Geddes and historians such as Lewis Mumford, urbanists such as Jane Jacobs, Bettencourt, and Geoffrey West are the founding fathers of urban mathematics, which demonstrates how urban infrastructures provide increasing returns (every marginal kilometer costs less) as do the resulting externalities (positive and negative). This allows us to predict that as a city grows:

– the amount of energy it uses for transportation (of people and goods) grows more than proportionally to the population, but so do its positive (economic opportunities and the potential for innovation) and negative (crime and pollution) externalities;

– how much the relation between its social efficiency and the energy lost due to transportation improves will depend on the quality of its connection, with energy and connection being closely correlated.

---

4 According to the definition given by the *Association Française d'Ingénierie Système* (French Systems Engineering Association): "A system of systems results from the collaborative operation between component systems which can function autonomously to complete their own operational tasks. The point of this collaboration is to highlight new exploited behaviors to improve the capacity of each component system or offer new ones, while maintaining the operational and managerial independence of all component systems". These systems can have heterogeneous behavioral laws which obey the laws of physics (such as *smart grids*) as well as human systems, the operation of which cannot be modeled by the laws of physics.

Controlling only physical parameters will quickly lead to impasses (losing on the one side what we gain on the other). If we consider a city as a complex living ecosystem of social relations, we will consider the intelligence of said city from interactions that residents can maintain among themselves: **designing a city becomes a problem of modeling complex systems**, more specifically, modeling a system of systems.

3.3. Smart territory

When the Chinese look back at their urban development policies, a recurring criticism is that they neglected China's social and cultural heritage and mimicked the Western development model, which produced inhumane and polluting cities. Both the lessons of the dysfunctional urbanization of the 19th and 20th Centuries and ongoing pilot projects demonstrate that a city cannot be designed in isolation from its territory and that it needs to be rooted in a territory that provides history and social capital.

3.3.1. *Territory: an immaterial asset*

Economic research into territories performed over the last couple of decades [AYD 86] demonstrates the importance of territorial **immaterial assets**, at the core of which is *social capital*, which contributes to building an *innovative environment* that will grant a competitive advantage. Today, this is a point that is present neither in corporate strategies nor in territorial reindustrialization policies. The OECD [OEC 14] is currently developing the concept of *smart specialization* that aims to identify territorial expertise around *enabling technologies* using the Porter model. The idea is to encourage businesses to identify a territory's traditional expertise and the benefits of a technology of a new scientific breakthrough. This model recognizes the role of endogenous growth and the principle of increasing returns tied to learning processes, as well as the territorialized accumulation of knowledge. This is an unusual approach with these types of institutions bound by the rules of standard economics that ignore the principle of increasing returns. Thus, European territorial funding (EFDR) will be replaced with specific funding for these territorialized *enabling technologies*. The Regional Center of France is currently serving as a test subject for this type of implementation. It is important that businesses integrate this into their strategies.

Designing smart cities cannot occur independently of territorial characteristics. Identifying a city's dynamic of "innovative environment" will play a critical role in the success of modeling, according to the concept developed by Philippe Aydalot. Its anthropological dimensions – history, culture, demographics, etc. – contribute to a *social intelligence*, which is one of the parent disciplines of competitive intelligence developed by Stevan Dedidjer. This will play a critical role in the success of modeling once the fact that residents are at the core of smart cities as producers and receivers of information, artifact users, and ultimately the ones that choose which equipment to use has been integrated into a city's development. The ecosystem's approach responds to the needs of a sustainable society organized around the common good.

In his particularly brilliant thesis [HUR 13], Philippe Hurdebourcq, researcher and director of a regional Chamber of Commerce and Industry in France, identified and formalized **three dimensions of a smart territory**, which is first and foremost an innovative environment. The first dimension of this environment is a network of stakeholders located on the same territory – geographic proximity – utilizing information technologies to help connect to organizational networks beyond the geographic territory. The second dimension aggregates expertise and technologies, which is a territory's cognitive capital. The territorial dynamic, if it functions, will mobilize this capital to perform the transition of an obsolete technological cycle towards the integration of new technologies. The third dimension is of course cooperation within these networks, which gives birth to local productive systems (LPS)[5]. These territorial logics help create external economies, agglomeration economies and, often, help open economies up to external markets because they offer businesses a sufficient critical size to consider sharing tertiary industrial services (R&D, marketing, communication, etc). Smart territories inherently produce a cycle of positive innovation that reinforces the appeal of the territory, which in turn reinforces the LPS by incorporating new players.

---

5 For the DATAR, a local productive system is defined as "*a productive organization located on a territory generally corresponding to an employment pool. This organization operates as a network of interdependences composed of productive units that have similar or complementary activities which divide the work (production or service companies, research centers, formation organisms, transfer centers and technological monitoring, etc.)*".

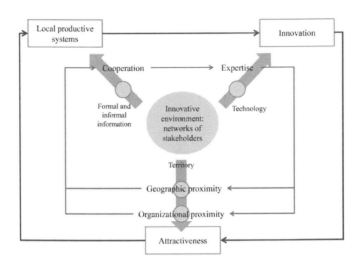

Figure 3.5. *The three dimensions of the innovative environment according to Philippe Hurdebourcq*

One of the surprising elements of the meticulous investigation lead by Philippe Hurdebourcq is that entrepreneurs, when they are even empirically aware of the nature of the territory and inherent advantages it provides, remain attached to a common discourse on the material benefits. Such benefits can include factors of attractiveness shared with public stakeholders, which in practice prevent territorial stakeholders from capitalizing their advantages as a smart territory. Figure 3.6 shows the falsehood of such a notion.

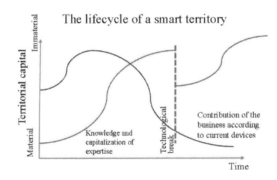

Figure 3.6. *Lifecycle of the smart territory and management strategy*

The administrative devices based on attractiveness of material advantages will begin by increasing through learning, capitalizing on expertise (immaterial capital) on which the territory can rely during the transition from one technological cycle to another, thus avoiding adaptation crises. However, these devices are not geared towards making a case for increasing the social capital and a territory's immaterial capital. This notion is actually barely taken into account in local development strategies, which always fail to consider the four types of advantage a territory can have:

– Two forms of *tangible* capital:

- **physical capital**, or natural capital, is a tangible resource that is non-transferrable and inimitable, such as a strategic geographic position, the presence of natural resources or the beauty of a site. A disadvantaged site will have to create other assets to become appealing, something we see with the old mining basins in Northern France, which recreate their territorial dynamic through other means than their industrial past within a natural environment that is not particularly appealing. This also includes the ecosystems that absorb and destroy waste and have a maximum processing capacity, which rich countries, in accordance with the Summers doctrine, circumvent by exporting their waste to poor countries;

- **material capital**, including infrastructures, buildings, machines and hard technologies, has a low mobility but is easily transferrable via reproduction. It constitutes a barrier to entry simply due to the volume of the required investment.

– Two forms of *intangible* capital:

- **intellectual capital** is more complex. There is formal intellectual capital, which is that of residents and institutions. There is a certain mobility to this element since it can be moved with people, or by replicating institutions like when a university creates an international branch. However, there is also a dimension to this that is rooted to the territory, first of all because people are not as mobile as predominant ideologies would suggest [FLO 02][6] and secondly because abilities and expertise reproduce idiosyncratically: the more one learns, the more that person is conditioned by what he or she has learnt and knowledge is placed into an institutional

6 See the empirical refutation of Richard Florida's theses on the mobility of the "creative classes" in Chapter 1.

context of rules that favor innovation or not. Great minds can be attracted to a territory with *brain drain* strategies – France has an advantage here thanks to the quality of life of its territories – but these will have to take root in a host territory. Intellectual capital is therefore only reproducible over a long period of time – it takes at least a generation for newcomers to take root – and on the condition that they enter a symbiotic relation with local knowledge;

	Easy to reproduce	Difficult to reproduce
Tangible resources	Material capital	Natural capital
Intangible resources	Intellectual capital	Social capital

Figure 3.7. *The four forms of capital in the composition of a territory*

- **social capital** represents the collective value of all of the social networks and incentives to do something for one another. It is the wealth of transactions between individuals and social groups, which represents fodder for innovation and social and civic life. It is typically this *atmosphere*, identified by Alfred Marshall at the end of the 19th Century as an immaterial asset of the territory that favors risk-taking and rewards entrepreneurial success. It affects natural solidarities and work relations, it has a built-in conflict resolution system, it allows collective professional action and it is able to push social and socio-technical consensuses forward. It is therefore a semi-natural ecosystem that finds its roots in history, allows survival over time and helps manage technical market changes.

3.3.2. *The territory secretes innovation (and not the other way around)*

The environment is therefore not homogenous, as standard economics seemed to suggest. It does not consist of a neutral support for production activities, which impact a company's decision on a location in the form of transportation costs that affect the flow of goods from where they are produced to where they are consumed or used. It is not just a support function for a function of production. The territory appears as a living entity, which is able to protect its businesses and provide them with a competitive advantage that allows them to be competitive at an international scale. In addition, unlike what used to be the case, the territory does not do this solely via its natural resources, or more generally, through its *generic resources* the value of which could be considered as independent from their production process or a company's expertise, which is, in that case, likely to behave predatorily, since it could consider that they may be acquired in any location under market conditions. This is the criticism that Gabriel Colletis makes of the French government's policy, which has *"always proceeded with a vision of the industry in question, not as global system (marked by the density of relations between businesses and/or other institutions such as universities, research centers) but as a simple sum of businesses. French industrial policy, unlike German industrial policy, has never sought to take into account the interdependencies between sectors within what could be considered a productive system"* [COL 12]. Confidence, networks, and an atmosphere favorable to innovation are a selection of the non-standardizable and non-copyable processes that compose a territory's sustainable competitive advantage.

For Philipe Aydalot [AYD 85], the territory is what offers its economic stakeholders the ability to secrete innovation. He considers that the territory is a partner to a business, just the same as a client, supplier employee, or a shareholder. By establishing collaborative relations between its local stakeholders, a business can contribute to reducing transaction costs, establish a climate of mutual trust and reduce the risks and information costs that go with that, while increasing their respective competitiveness and providing irrecoverable gain. This will thus solidify their position through their immaterial, cognitive, ethical or organizational inputs.

Conversely to the theories of Richard Florida, **it is the territory that creates innovation** and not the import of the social capital of the supposed "creative classes" in a territory strictly enclosed into an urban space. For Philippe Aydalot *"an innovative business does not pre-exist its environment, on the contrary it is secreted by it"*. The territory is generally an immaterial capital which is characterized by a number of factors: history and an ability to generate a common project; the ability to generate consensuses, which is correlated with the dynamic of innovation; *immaterial* *territorial assets,* such as the access to technological knowledge; the composition of the job-market; and a technical expertise that makes up the three components of an **innovative environment**. Through its characteristics, this environment generates innovation of any sort. We identify three dimensions within this (Figure 3.5):

– **Local production systems** are characterized by their proximity to production units, which maintain more or less intense relations. These businesses can be members of the same sector, have similar expertise or share a similar product, and be confined to the same region or employment pool. The novelty of *i*conomics is that geographic proximity can be complemented (but not replaced) with digital networks. It allows pooling, development and innovation by creating a network-like dynamic.

– These LPS produce **innovation** in the sense that Schumpeter meant it, i.e. new combinations among products, services and technologies. Producing these combinations and integrating new technologies into old diminishing returns ones helps revitalize old industrial pools. French steelwork was a mono-industry heavily territorialized onto mining sites. In going from a focus on tons of product – its old performance metric (which was the case for all extraction activities) – to a metric that could be measured in gigabytes contained in the steel they were producing, it introduced an immaterial dimension to its added value and stimulated the diversification of activities around its production sites.

– **Territorial appeal**, which neoclassic economics claims to be purely composed of low salaries or fiscal dumping. The appeal of an industrial area is not its price per square meter, but the synergies offered by its networks. Specialized in precision cutting software for the textile industry, the company *Lectra System* did not give in to the siren songs of outsourcing in search of low salaries during the textile crisis. On the contrary, it stood fast in its little town in Gironde near Bordeaux to bet on the dynamism of the local networks creating more value than savings made on salaries from employees reduced to no more than automatons.

3.3.3. *The territorial dynamic in action*

The **Choletais** region, around the city of Cholet, specializes in off-the-rack clothing and shoe manufacturing – two declining industries – but has succeeded in converting itself to *i*conomics, something that governmental projects that sought to group businesses together and make them "global scale companies" failed to do. The region was able to achieve this thanks to the quality of their social capital with economic actors showing solidarity to one another ("no-layoff" practices) and policies rooted in social Christianity that stimulated synergies among companies, cities, rural workshops and training devices. The two sectors of activity present in the Choletais – clothing and shoe manufacturing – entered phases of diminishing returns back in the 1960s. The textile industry received government input and focused on making global-sized companies, while the shoe industry mobilized its network of sub-contractors to reinvent itself to face the competition from Asia that was flooding the markets with shoes that were of the price at which the Choletais was buying their leather. The quality of the interactions within the territory allowed them to use their technological assets and target high-end markets. Beginning in 2004, all activities within the Choletais were uniting within a cluster organized into subsets of businesses around a common theme: children. This is the only cluster in France to be organized into a market theme rather than an industrial sector.

The **Swiss watchmaking industry,** faced with the shocking appearance of the digital watch – which potentially announced the death of the watchmaking industry – was able to utilize its expertise – high-precision micromechanics – and reuse it for neighboring sectors such as fabricating prosthetic hips. This restarted a local industrial fabric thanks to the interdependence among industrial sectors and a culture of common cooperation. On the other side of the Jura Mountains, French companies did not enjoy the same atmosphere and suffered from a lack of solidarity between industrial clients and policies that favored large-scale research rather than valuing the ability for innovation of personnel. These industries did not experience the same social climate.

The **territorial dynamic**, continues Bernard Pecqueur [PEC 07], creates a prosperity founded on endogenous elements (their specificity) and exogenous elements (their ability to fit into the world economy). In a general sense, "*the adoption of organizational models based on the horizontal decentralization of services at the expense of vertical hierarchical models ensures a better reactivity in the face of changing economic and technological environments*", says François Caron, a reference author in the field of innovation history [CAR 12].

The intelligence of a city cannot be considered separately from the intelligence of the territory and results from the convergence of a number of spheres (Figure 3.2): the *atmosphere* of the territory, which favors risk-taking, with rich interactions among individuals allows the territory to evolve over time; and the *industrial dynamic*: the more an industry is rooted in its territory, the more it develops specific competitive advantages resulting from interdependences with the local fabric which, for example, make cost-based outsourcings pointless. An industrial offer to produce a smart city cannot simply be a sum of technologies but must look for synergies through the principle of coopetition[7].

In the given examples, these ecosystems formed naturally depending on historical and cultural factors. However, can we encourage this dynamic and combine top-down public policy with bottom-up organic decision-making?

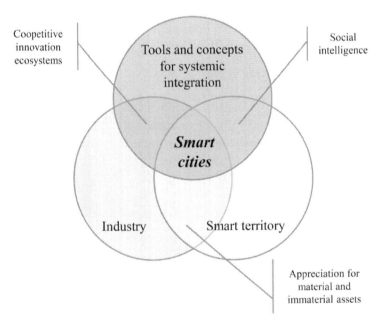

Figure 3.8. *Smart city as a system integrated with its territory*

---

7 Coopetition: need for companies to simultaneously compete and cooperate in order to define global offerings.

Countries that come from an authoritarian and centralizing tradition such as Russia and China are taking an interest in these approaches. This does not seem to be the case for France, which appears to be totally set on centralization and metropolization.

3.4. Are metropolises smart territories?

In the early 1990s, urbanization born from the industrial revolution was growing in a context where the world was becoming more and more internationalized and globalized [DUM 15] under the form of a metropolization process which sociologist Saskia Sassen described as the *global city*, born of a paradoxical dynamic: on the one hand, the widespread outsourcing and relocation of the production of goods and, on the other hand, the centralization of globalized coordination, prediction and management functions. Thus, the more international the economy gets, the greater the control functions of large businesses conglomerate to a handful of sites. In 1991, Saskia Sassen identified only three global cities capable of commanding the international economy: Tokyo, New York and London. The University of Loughborough created criteria for classifying cities according to their degree of integration into the world economy, with two cities at the top: London and New York[8].

These giant cities grow under the principle that large agglomerations provide increasing returns because they offer a wider employment market and have the ability to offer diverse infrastructures that respond to the needs of globalized businesses: international airports, business centers, and higher and higher bandwidths for digital networks. Globalized business in turn favors large cities, where the costs of these types of equipment are easily recouped and, therefore, they become profitable faster. Furthermore, major cities offer advantages that go with "agglomeration economies" that result from the concentration of certain functions: research and design, intellectual services, intercompany commerce, management or culture and activities. Nonetheless, there is not an automatic advantage for populated agglomerations to grow superior in terms of appeal and innovation. The latter also depends on the quality of territorial governance and the climate,

---

8 This ranking is updated every 4 years on GaWC (Globalization and World Cities), http://www.lboro.ac.uk/gawc/group.html.

which can be more or less favorable to entrepreneurship. These criteria make a *smart territory*.

Furthermore, due to their high density in terms of population and activity, large cities also suffer from what is known as dis-economies of scale, once past their G* spot[9]: property costs, time wasted in transports, pollution, criminality and stress. The combination of these factors that are favorable and unfavorable to metropolization occurs in favor of certain cities and not in others. Paris, for instance, has lost a number of decision-centers in the past few years.

In addition, lastly, we are noticing in France, in Europe, and throughout the world that a number of companies with international clientele, rather than seeking out major cities at all costs, are remaining or moving to medium-sized cities or even small towns. Any territory can be valued because it is not just a geographic space, but a living space which holds potential [MIC 13]. In addition, it is a fact that, in France, businesses are created in territories – medium-sized cities not just and not large ones[10].

As for innovation, while it is true that the effects of synergies linked to the proximity between universities, businesses and research centers can be interesting, they are in no way exclusive. Innovation stems from entrepreneurship more than it does from a placement in a big city, as we saw in the examples of the Choletais and the Swiss watchmaking industry, which explain the multiple innovations appearing outside of the cities.

G.F Dumont states that the French Parliament appears to be reproducing the top-down administrative procedure used by Soviet Russia, believing that simply granting the title of "metropolis" to a territory, created as a public agency, redistributing certain competencies between territorial collectives while re-centralizing power is enough to create dynamism, which is an illusion. While the size of a territory is negligible in its impact on appeal or innovation, it would be more important to improve the conditions that allow unified access to better territorial governance.

The result of metropolization is the acceleration of urban gentrification: rising house prices in city centers turned playground for the

---

9 See next chapter.

10 Conjunctural note by Trendeo for 2017 http://www.trendeo.net/conjoncture-septembre-2017-reprise-se-poursuit-lindustrie/.

"creative classes", a belt of *low cost* and "useless" immigrants for all small jobs required by the gentrifiers, and the expulsion of the old working classes to the outskirts where they can die and be forgotten. Metropolization comes from the concept of *Global City* and spreads inequalities, poverty and distress among the under-qualified, spreading the death of territories wherever it goes. All of this under the cool aspect of the "creative classes": Zola's *Rougon Macquarts* are now disguised as hipsters [GUI 16].

3.5. A city is not a collection of smarties

In October 2012, at the Eurocities forum in Vienna, a member of the "smart transportation" group of the European Union Mobility Directorate pointed out that none of the pilot projects financed in recent years by the European Commission had yet been formalized or even reproduced. The goal of systemic modeling is precisely to be able to measure the impacts of an endogenous or exogenous change by charting the links between the variables and parameters of an ecosystem.

Intelligence does not come from the sum of communication systems that lead us to *"unite the separate as separate"* (Guy Debord) or to *"live alone together"* (J.P Lebrun), but from the interactions that serve to generate social bonds and learning. The systemic analysis approach developed by Michael Batty will accentuate the relations between the different elements of a city. These elements will constitute networks connected by activity flows. The element itself is not what is smart, but rather the connection and the networks: to understand a city, we must understand its flows, the objective being to be able to predict the evolution of these flows and networks. This is precisely the goal of new urban sciences that attempt not to remain on the surface of things, but rather to understand how a city operates, how it is more than a collection of physical elements, and how it behaves like a living organism.

3.5.1. *A city is a living system...*

Historically, cities were identified by economy analysts as places where synergies developed between activities with increasing returns. Neapolitan Antonio Serra, in a book that paved the way for modern economics, compares Venice, a city with no land for agriculture, and Naples, a city which has an abundance of it. Venice has been a sustainable city thanks to the synergies between its industrial activities (including naval construction), its merchant activities and its military power. It began declining when the pole of the developed world shifted from the Mediterranean to the Atlantic. At the other end, Naples, seat of the viceroy to the Spanish throne with great agricultural wealth and money from the New World, was unable to reimagine itself and leave feudalism.

The interaction between a city and its environment was modeled by Johan Heinrich von Thünen in the 19th Century: at the center of the city are the strongest synergies between activities with increasing returns – industrial activities – then six concentric areas organize the activities with gradually diminishing returns – primary and service activities – and the transportation costs increase, defining a boundary which Fernand Braudel called a "world economy".

With the second industrial revolution at the end of the 19th Century, city development became guided primarily by the quest for returns to scale, at the expense of social solidarities and civic life, as analyzed by Emile Durkheim in *The Division of Labour in Society* (1893).

3.5.2. ...which we understand today through new approaches...

Geoffrey West's mathematics of the city[11] provides a scientific support for Jane Jacobs's empirical intuition that insisted on the necessary "village" dimension that should be maintained to allow for creative interactions between residents and their activities and to use social capital efficiently. Jacobs [JAC 85] considers that wealth is not produced by the accumulation of urban assets (such as large operations of urban renovations), but with the ability of residents to engage in the production of said assets and the urban system's ability to adapt to changing circumstances. The error of urban policies, she says, has been rationalizing cities and adapting them for a few functions by importing others, whereas wealth is created by the interaction of all urban activities, considered unprofitable as standalone, and advocating the substitution of imports from outside the city via the means of diversified urban activities.

---

11 See Chapter 4.

What highlights the critical point when modeling this system is the border between the city and its outskirts. It is essential, on the one hand, since by definition a system is differentiated from its environment by a border (without which it would not exist and would be ungovernable), which defines what is "within" it and what is "outside" it, representing exogenous parameters, the number of which and the variance of which define the turbulence of the environment. This boundary must characterize the urban ecosystem in that it is coherent and stable, creating wealth through internal activities and importing only what makes sense to import. Furthermore, on a material level, a city's extension exists within a geographic context. Before the second industrial revolution and the development of telecommunications, cities and their outskirts were structured by the distance measured by the speed of information – a man on a horse, then a boat and then a railway. The second industrial revolution allowed, for the first time, the "death of distance" making distance no longer the structuring element of these territorial ecosystems and the end of the "Thünen zones". The consequence has been the "oil-slick" urban growth along with energy consumption and the development of a dysfunctional urbanization, denounced by Jane Jacobs, in housing, work and administrative functions.

The "death of distance" means that Thünen zones can extend to the entire world[12]. Cities will concentrate on high added-value activities, while activities that pollute a lot and have poor working conditions are rejected far into the outskirts. This way, even if a city may appear to be "green" within its administrative perimeter, the evaluation of its ecosystem must include the externalities of outsourced activities. For instance, the carbon footprint of a "green city" must include its imported CO_2: a city may be green but its ecosystem dark grey (Figure 5.17).

3.5.3. ...at the heart of which the sciences of complexity...

An ecosystem is the number of dynamic sub-systems in constant interaction (energy management systems, transport systems, water management systems, social systems, climate ecosystems, residents,

12 The commune of Séné (Morbihan, Brittany), instead of choosing to use Breton granite, chose to import Chinese granite to reconstruct its main artery.

facilities, etc.), and which interact with their collective environment while maintaining the ability to preserve their identity and improve their internal diversity. In the evolution of natural ecosystems, they schematically go through three types, from type I that finds its resources and rejects its waste into its environment, to type III that recycles completely just like the biosphere [AYR 96]. The idea of an "ecological engineering" that would allow us to create "viable industrial strategies" inspired by natural ecosystems was formulated in 1989 [FRO 89]. An industrial ecosystem can never attain stage III due to the entropic nature of the economic process [GEO 70]. Its design requires specific modeling and architectural skills that link disciplines with abilities spread out through different companies in a common architecture.

One application of this approach is illustrated by the constraints imposed on Chinese eco-cities. An ecosystem differs from a system in that the interactions between its different internal elements make it capable of reproducing or even producing (as is the case in autopoietic systems) the rules of its operation as a whole or in part.

3.5.4. ...help conjugate internal semi-stability and external instability

The choice of the border of the system is therefore critical in the eyes of the problem in question, which is a key point in the engineering of complex systems: defining what is "within" and what is "outside". In the ideal types of Thünen zones, each zone has a specific function and defined interactions with its neighboring zones, in the order of decreasing complexity from the center towards the outskirts, the whole thing making a sustainable ecosystem since the Thünen model allows very little to no exchanges with the outside. In real life, this system would be subject to destabilizing actions from the outside that would threaten the internal equilibrium of the ecosystem.

Another essential characteristic of the sustainable urban ecosystem, just like natural ecosystems [HOL 73], is its *resilience*, or the ability to learn and to adapt to rapid fluctuations in its environment, including crises and disasters, and generate new rules that will allow it to face an increase in external turbulence. The school of High-Reliability Organizations, started by

Karlene Roberts [ROB 90], helps define organizational traits in terms of process design, information circulation and processing, understanding and mastering human factors, and governance systems to allow sustainability in the organization in a turbulent environment including foreseeable yet unpredictable disasters (marine submersion, seismic activity, terrorism, etc.).

Today we have a rich body of operational research surrounding organizations facing uncertainty with the works of Christian Morel on *absurd decisions* [MOR 12]. We talk about an absurd decision when there is a radical disproportion between the reference rationality of an individual or a group and the objective they wish to achieve. One classic example is the application of a procedure that is designed for the situation of a given complexity to a far more complex one. These mistakes are purely human and rely on procedures and systems designed by people, which lead to radical and persistent errors. The first works by Christian Morel started with the observation of the frequency with which US surgeons operate on the wrong side of a patient. The risk for error increases dramatically in emergency or crisis situations where the ability to think is sometimes absent.

One of the reasons that the residents of the city of Christchurch, New Zealand, refused to have their city rebuilt by a central agency following its destruction from a series of earthquakes in 2011 was precisely that such an agency cannot integrate all the parameters of the complexity created by an earthquake, and that such an approach would sterilize the capacity for initiative of the city's residents. Once we know that the earthquakes will come back, if we want the city to be resilient, the residents must be granted the ability to establish and manage scenarios which prepare them to react to the unexpected and increase the population's competency. The city nominated a *Chief Resilience Officer* and, since 2016, dedicates 10% of its budget to reinforcing its resilience. The idea is that social phenomena (homelessness, poverty, flooding and natural disasters) are not isolated events, but rather global interconnected phenomena that constitute an attack on the system that must be able to respond in its entirety.

These considerations help define the road map to developing the abilities of actors within a smart city. The critical abilities are therefore those of architects and engineers of complex systems and the attribution of these abilities this ability to a central controller who will navigate the interactions between architectural abilities and sub-system proprietors. This, of course, is the complete opposite of IBM's *Big Brother* in Rio de Janeiro. The role of this controller is not to do everything, but to animate a design process of meta-rules of operation for a city, a collective intelligence shared by each actor. The roles and prerogatives of local actors must be defined, and the latter must be considered as part of a collective thought process and a creative energy that is difficult if not impossible to model, but which must be accounted for by higher rank systems. The sustainable city includes a definition of the architecture of abilities and roles. This ability will primarily develop with civil planners, and also in company business models, in order to integrate optimization metrics of the whole city and not just the company.

3.6. The dangers of a technocentric approach

The first evident danger is the dependence created towards technology providers. It is not practicable to give up these technologies. The barriers to entry for creating a competing industry are astronomical. There are the costs of investment for building infrastructures, and also market penetration, which would require integrated exclusively compatible interlocks similar to what Bill Gates created when he joined Windows and Intel: the soft and the hard, software and machine. However, it is not forbidden to manage these power balances. France's major companies gathered within the CIGREF[13] to regulate their profession. Cities setting off into the adventure of smart cities would be well advised to create such clubs in order to develop their lacking digital skills, on the one hand, and share their experiences on the other hand.

Furthermore, in the ruthless world of this new market, soft power strategies set the pace. Soft power aims to create an ideology that conforms to the interests of the dominant party, to which subordinates adhere out of conviction. This is something much more powerful than hard power – a coup d'etat, bombings, invasions – which are reserved for those who refuse to

---

13 *Club Informatique des Grandes Entreprises Françaises*. CIGREF is a French association of public and private companies represented by their information systems directors (CIOs) who have concluded a series of agreements with vendors to normalize their relations with clients, beginning with "updating" and "new versions" practices, which are heavily priced to corporations and are often just programmed obsolescence.

adopt "Western values". These ideologies take the appearance of rational evidence, which claims to rely on science, as is the case with neo-liberal economics, or noble causes such as the climate or the environment. This is how myths appear, which are hard to resist under penalty of being excluded from networks of influence and jeopardy to one's career. These myths have their temples and their mass: the Davos forum where world leaders gathered in 2015, renting 1,700 private jets, to discuss the climate change[14]. They have their guru, Jeremy Rifkin, whose theories could easily have been included in the smoke and mirrors section of this book. Rifkin predicts the third industrial revolution in the convergence between digital and renewable energies and maintains that energy can be produced by networking buildings with positive energy, which is entirely false[15] and dangerous. Rifkin ignores the dangers of the digital, which he considers as a common good, the marginal cost of which is null, omitting data collection, risks of intrusion and destabilization strategies, and ignores the external costs of renewable energies (the perimeter of which is limited to wind turbines and solar energy that are being invested in by large companies and ignoring all others), which make them – in their current state of development – more costly and polluting than fossil fuels[16]. Moreover, it works: Rifkin sold a "master plan" for 350,000 euros to the Nord Pas de Calais region for managing its "energy transition". The road to the smart city is littered with pitfalls and cunning opportunists who will seduce naive or lazy leaders who lack the culture and critical thought to prevent them from rushing into the latest trend.

From a functional standpoint, the technocentric approach does not account for its users – or sees its typical user as disconnected from any culture or territory – when they are the gauge for reliability when designing technical systems, as authors such as Gilbert Simondon and Eric von Hippel have demonstrated. It is up to the user to adapt to the tool and not the tool to adapt to the functional needs of the user. The technocentric approach does not account for a territorial, social or historical context. It considers that the territory is a null value and it is created by the power of the *Deus ex machina* that is a machine.

---

14 *L'Express*, 10/21/2015. Specifically, they do not only discuss the climate: in this forum that charges $40,000 to enter they also discuss wage inequality, and this assembly composed of 83% men also discusses inequality towards women.

15 See [PRU 17]. For a scientific analysis of the third industrial revolution, see [REI 12].

16 For an analysis of Rifkin's theories, see Gadrey [GAD 13].

Finally, and this is very serious, it does not take into account the statute of data, which becomes critical with the development of *Big Data*, which we will look at more closely at the end of this book. Data have progressively moved from "data confidentiality" (which is a fundamental right) to "data property" (which is a market). These data are processed by powerful algorithms, which function thanks to a high-level mathematical language that only a handful of experts are able to audit. Data property and its processing will be the fundamental critical point of the smart city.

The approach of the smart city through modeling complex systems will allow us to chart all of these phenomena, to highlight these interactions; the desired and undesired effects and the exiting from the scientism of the ideology of the *smart city*.

4

New Sciences of Cities

Unlike medieval cities, which constituted an archetype of an integrated system, the cities of the 20th Century gradually structured themselves around single functions. The pollution resulting from industrialization brought on a disassociation between habitat functions and production functions. In addition, and more importantly, the post-war reconstruction era saw the emergence of "machines for living in", which were unifunctional and separate from industrial areas: the "machines for making". In order to leave this unhealthy type of urbanism, we must return to an urbanism which strives to have life in the city in all of its components and which does not only optimize a few parameters, and not just those of promoters.

Succeeding in this integration of a city's dimensions requires an understanding of how a city lives and evolves, and then an ability to model these dynamics. Research surrounding urban dynamics is old and dates back to Lewis Mumford, but it has recently experienced resurgence with the *sciences of cities*, including the works of Michael Batty, *The New Science of Cities* [BAT 13], which is an attempt to integrate all components of a city's simulation and define the roles of its actors. Lewis Mumford, Patrick Geddes and Jane Jacobs were the first and harshest critics of the "oil-slick" urbanism of American cities, which resulted in the formation of urban *conurbation*s, a notion coined by Patrick Geddes to refer to urbanized zones outside of a historical urban core which connect major cities to one another as a result of the definitive death of distance, but which are not being actual cities.

The idea is therefore to reform a definition and a dynamic of cities which allows us to escape the fatality of oil-slick growth. It is a recent science, explains Michael Batty, which was born during the 20th Century thanks to

Patrick Geddes (1915–1949) and which really found its stride in the early 21st Century. The fundamental idea is that cities must be considered as constellations of interactions, communications, relations, flows and networks rather than physical locations, since the latter is simply the synthesis of these interactions.

Cities do not exist outside of their environment and cannot be cut off from the vastness of the world. They are *never in equilibrium*. They are constantly changing and after changing they remain *far from the equilibrium*. They do not obey a central top-down order, but evolve from the bottom-up as the product of the decisions of millions of individuals and groups, and sometimes intersect with central decisions. This complementarity between proliferation and a decentralized life which produces an automatically organized life and a central impulse has become a central theme in research.

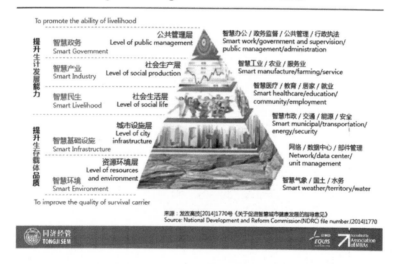

Figure 4.1. *The Chinese approach to urban integration. (Source: Quangbin Wang). For a color version of this figure, see www.iste.co.uk/rochet/cities.zip*

A smart city will result in the integration of *human* and *material* components. We can imagine it with the development of methods for engineering complex systems adapted to urban design, which rely on both physical and social sciences and allow us to understand the role played by residents in a city's evolution. Chinese planners have not wasted any time in integrating this system approach[1]: the advantage of this Chinese strategy is in looking at a city as a *whole* rather than a mere sum of its parts, accentuating the ability to integrate technologies which, for the time being, come from the Western world. Their approach understands that what controls the system controls the underlying technologies, and not the other way around.

4.1. The more or less sympathetic myths of the ideal city

A city has always been a petri dish for myths surrounding research for the perfect city. The first exercise was performed by Thomas More with *Utopia* (1516). In this book, he denounced religious intolerance and set the scene of an idealized world in which all citizens could find happiness. Private property does not exist. Obligatory work ensures general prosperity. In addition, liberty of the cult is guaranteed there. The title itself is a neologism from the Greek for "a place which does not exist", and expresses the idea that More did not really believe that this project could ever exist. Later, there was Tommaso Campanella (1568–1639), and the *City of the Sun*. Campanella was a Neapolitan monk and revolutionary who spent many years in prison. His model for a perfect city is a totalitarian existence. Everything there is ruled by the State which itself is a theocracy. In order to build the perfect citizens to inhabit the City of the Sun, rigorous eugenics are used to retain only perfect children, who receive an education which would make even modern teachers pale in comparison: the children's education occurs without violence, open to both abstract notions and learning trades, using images, field-trips and discoveries. For a perfect society, the condition is that people are seen as perfect and their lives regulated down to the slightest detail. There are no marriages but only pairings based on an astrological calendar in order to make perfect babies, who never know the passion of private property: everything is pooled together in the City of the Sun.

Campanella in turn inspired Robert Owen (1771–1858), who attempted to create harmonious communities for workers to escape the hell of

---

1 Presentation by Quangbin Wang, Faculty Head of the School of Economics and Management, Tongji University, at the international seminar on smart cities, Shanghai, China, October 2014.

working-class life during the first industrial revolution. He believed that scientific progress would, through education, create more rational men who were less controlled by their passions. Unlike More and Campanella, Robert Owen actually did create these utopic communities, which were to be the basis for a new social and political order. Owen wanted to change people, greedy capitalists and depraved alcoholic laborers alike. To change them, he had to change the city, because people are a result of their environment. He created his ideal city of New Lanarck, which received exceptional results and was visited by great minds from around the world. Working-class children were schooled from a young age, something unique in England, on the conviction that a healthy and educated laborer would be more productive than a beast of burden. Nonetheless, Owen considered that the working class, in its current state, was unfit to govern itself and that the truth should be passed on down to it from above by an enlightened elite. Owen lacked any notion of a city based on organic growth.

With Charles Fourier in France (1772–1837), utopia becomes even more precise with the creation of phalansteries. However, Fourier expects nothing from the people; he designs his doctrine as a social science that is mostly concerned with carrying out experiments to try out his theories. What all these approaches have in common is the idea that knowledge of the laws of human behavior would allow us to design the perfect city which forces people to behave. A perfect city for perfect people.

This notion can take us down a rabbit hole, and not necessarily to where we might expect. Frédéric Rouvillois is the author of a book [ROU 14] on the link between Nazism and utopia. He highlights that the common denominator between all utopias is their ambition to build in the here and now, using science and technique, a perfect society, an ideal city, bespoke and in service of the new citizen. A paradise on Earth which will translate to a general reconciliation: conciliation between humankind and nature, conciliation between all people. The theme of equality is ever-present, not because equality is inherently good, but because it helps eliminate the need for and possibility of conflict. A utopia is the disappearance of conflict and randomness: it is a world without friction – *seamless* is the phrase current smart city theorists keep repeating – which supposes a stranglehold on all beings, nature and history. Nazism follows a tradition of Campanella's utopic eugenics. Nazism found its origin in German romanticism, in the story of a supposed perfect primitive Germanic society that learned societies such as Thulé have found hard to find. The father of modern anti-Semitism is Theodor Fritsch, who in 1896 published the first book on garden cities *Die Stadt der Zukunft*, the city of the future. He intended to fight the scourges of modern life, of big city life, a source of the disappearance of German values and the propagation of vice. The garden city must provide a harmonious frame of a medium-sized city promoting the values of local produce, which will push back against the "corruptive" forces of the stateless Jews. Unluckily for him, he died in 1933 just after the Nazis rose to power and paid him homage.

We know of Hitler's taste for urbanism from his closeness with one of his ministers, Albert Speer, and his project to build a new capital, Germania, which would illustrate the power of new Germany. However, Hitler, and indeed, Himmler, also had a fascination for the ideal of a small city of 20,000 people, united by small commune values and life that could monitor one another.

All of these theories and experiences had in common the *perfect city for perfect people*, designed using pseudo-scientific theories held by superior individuals, a city where conflict would disappear.

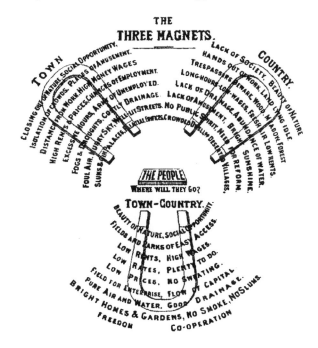

Figure 4.2. *The three magnets that structure the city, according to Ebenezer Howard*

This does not hold true for the real theorist behind the garden cities, British writer Ebenezer Howard [HOW 02], who started out with a goal to remedy the filth in the streets of London in the late 19th Century. The garden city is a synthesis of city and countryside (Figure 4.2). Howard suggested we build cities no bigger than 30,000 people, surrounded by agricultural lands which would prevent them from growing like the oil-slick cities. Each city could only grow by building other similar cities, all linked by easy communication systems. The ancestor of today's urban clusters, the garden city is but the prime unit in a vast world. Factories located on the outskirts of each city would provide work for residents, and save them from long trips. Howard shared the utopist idea of "bringing the people back to the land", which carried real values.

There were two instances of garden cities built – Letchworth and Welwyn – but they never succeeded in decongesting London.

Howard's approach is largely appreciated. Lewis Mumford claims it to be the only true attempt to build an organic city. However, Jane Jacobs criticized it harshly: *"He [Howard] conceived of good planning as a series of static acts; in each case the plan must anticipate all the needed... He was uninterested in the aspects of the city that could not be abstracted to serve his utopia"* [JAC 61]. As noted by Dennis Hardy, a historian of urban utopias, Howard attempted to build a perfect city in an imperfect world, while utopists believe in building a perfect city in a perfect world [HAR 91]. Indeed, no matter the advantage of Howard's approach, it remained top-down planning. It never found the key to a truly organic dynamic, and the two cities he created resembled small Parisian suburbs, rather than the true cities that Howard envisioned.

What we should learn from urban utopias is that perfect cities cannot be built for perfect people. People are imperfect and attempting to change that leads to totalitarianism and eugenics under its different forms, and the perfect cities would be so only for a short period of time under given conditions, which, by their nature, will change. Understanding the systemic nature of cities remains the key to designing them in a way in which they can evolve from residents' true, imperfect, lives and habits.

4.2. A city is an imbalanced system

In summary, *cities are like biological organisms*, rather than mechanical machines. The evolution of sciences of complexity and systems theory from a top-down approach to a bottom-up approach allows us to consider the city as an open system that is the product of an evolving process, rather than a grand design which is the case for Baroque cities.

The new sciences of cities rely on the observation that cities are systems that grow from the bottom-up, as opposed to the traditional notion of cities designed from the top-down. Even if a city is founded by one individual (such as is the case for Saint Petersburg by Peter the First), it acquires its own autonomous life and develops organically, from the bottom-up – otherwise it will die. Most urban systems are not "built" but grown. They evolve through the multitude of decisions taken within them.

Originally, a city comes from the necessity for people to group together and to have economic and social relations – search for synergies – for either commercial, military or political purposes. This phenomenon can occur anywhere – we will study the cases of two very unlikely cities, Singapore and Norilsk – and the geographic distribution of cities is ostensibly egalitarian. While all cities start off with the same potential by creating connections, the latter are not universal, as explained by Herbert A. Simon, the founding father of design sciences: *"Everything is connected but some things are more connected than others. The world is a large matrix of interactions in which most of the entries are close to zero, and in which, by ordering those entries according to their orders of magnitude, a distinct hierarchic structure can be discerned..."* [SIM 77].

Then, certain cities develop more synergies and rise above the others. The larger cities begin to absorb the smaller ones. The important point is that the diversity of these cities obeys common principles of *modeling* and *scalability* (growth). They develop in fractals, meaning that they reproduce the same patterns.

By "model", we of course do not mean the lazy principle used by politicians when they talk about "models" – the "German, Swedish model..." – which is a simple imitation, a copy-and-paste, of a foreign experience. A model is an abstract representation of a reality that highlights recurring traits. No matter the city, it must deal with problems in relations between housing and workplace, energy flows, communications networks, etc. A model will outline recurring configurations, or *patterns* as Christopher Alexander calls them, libraries of rules to connect them. There are no two identical cities, but all cities have similar problems that can be understood and represented by models.

Let us begin by introducing the fundamental concepts of the necessary systemics to understanding a city.

4.2.1. *Definition of an urban ecosystem*

A **system** is a dynamic set of sub-systems in interaction with one another (water management systems, transportation systems, energy management, social systems, environmental ecosystems, residents, etc.) and interacts with its environment while being capable of maintaining its identity and improving its internal diversity.

The condition for a city to be smart is that it be treated as a **system of systems**, or a set of heterogeneous systems. They each have their autonomous systemic dynamic, but are in dynamic interaction with one another to create a *meta-system*. This meta-system is a system more complex than the sum of its sub-systems. In application of Ashby's law (see footnote 2, this chapter), the meta-system can govern its coordination. The exchange of information within a system of systems is therefore a critical point that supposes a common basis of information and an interoperability of data on a common schematic and syntax, or *meta-language.*

An **ecosystem** differs from a system in that it is capable, from the single interaction of its internal elements, to reproduce its rules of operation, or even produce new rules of operation, in full (as in the case of *autopoetic* systems) or in part. The ecosystem is therefore capable of evolving by itself.

By **urban ecosystem**, we mean, by analogy with the notion of a natural ecosystem, an ecosystem built by people integrating all elements that make up a city that interacts naturally among one another and with their environment, in a global state of imperfect equilibrium that enables the sustainability of the city in its exchanges with its environment: resource extraction, wealth and well-being creation, and waste management. The ecosystem is not sustainable in the sense that there would be no entropy. It can only be if there are activities that generate negative entropy (or negentropy) against the entropy generated by the environment. This entropy–negentropy relation can be identified and modeled by a system architecture.

In application of the law of requisite variety (or Ashby's law[2]), the bigger the number of parameters and variables, the more complex the ecosystems that can be designed, but then their operation will be harder to master. For example, the bigger the energy sources, the more we can define an "energy mix" to supply a city, the larger the diversity of architectures for ecosystems and the higher the complexity of governing such a mix.

The choice of a **system boundary** is therefore critical since the idea is to control the oil-slick outwards expansion of a city, and the development of conurbations that are neither city nor countryside, as denounced by Patrick Geddes, Lewis Mumford and Jane Jacobs. Something that defines a key task of complex systems' engineering is defining what is *within* and what is *outside*, and with those parameters, the size of a city. As we saw with Lewis Mumford's work, this was the great asset of medieval cities, which had systemic perimeters defined by a wall. In real life, this system will be subjected to destabilizing actions from the outside, some of which will threaten the internal equilibrium of the ecosystem. A system architect will attempt to model the reactions of not only foreseeable phenomena (such as environmental and financial events), but also unforeseeable ones. If the Fukushima power plant had been built on an elevated platform and the generator cooling systems had worked with water rather than air, the disaster could have been limited [JAM 11]. The risk of marine submersion, a low-probability event, but with a high impact, had therefore not been taken into account during design. The sustainable urban ecosystem, just like natural ecosystems, must similarly be *resilient.*

The **critical competency** is therefore that of architect and engineer of complex systems and a city's sustainability will rely on an architecture of abilities and roles distributed throughout sub-systems and their ability to co-evolve and coordinate with as little intervention from the center, the role of which would have to be limited to designing architecture rules and controlling certain large central systems.

---

2 Ashby's law states that the governance system of a complex system must be at least as complex as the governed system, and if not, the governance is inverted: one is no longer controlling the complexity, it is controlling you.

4.2.2. *A city is a system in incomplete equilibrium*

We owe Michael Batty for the first formalization of this new science, which considers that a city is not only a location, but also a *constellation of interactions,* of *activity flows and networks* in an open environment. **A city cannot be designed as a system in equilibrium,** as was attempted by the utopists of the 19th Century who wanted to remedy the damages done by the industrial revolution on the structure of the city, with the garden cities started by Ebenezer Howard. These cities were rigid systems that were unable to evolve, grow and diversify, the few examples of which, as nice as they were, did not survive. Batty defines a city as a system that is "far from equilibrium".

This means that the traditional approach to the representation of a city, through plans which define ideal configurations by imposing restrictions to unpredictable changing situations, is likely to be unsatisfactory and will not help understand the wealth of urban life.

The science of systems brings us back to an organic vision of a city's growth, ruled by a few laws which describe contradictory dynamics that illustrate this impossibility for a city to be in stationary equilibrium:

– **Metcalfe's law**, or the law of networks: the value of a network, or the *potential* number of connections it allows, grows from the square of the density of said network. We could be tempted to infer from this that the denser a city is, the more opportunities it offers, but...

– ... **von Thünen's model**, completed by geographic studies by Waldo Tobler, shows that the *real* number of connections decreases the further away from the center you get: *"Everything is related to everything else, but near things are more related than distant things"* (Tobler).

– **Marshall's law** (resulting from agglomeration effects studied by Marshall in the 19th Century) completed by calculations by **West and Bettencourt** [WES 07], who compiled data from all major cities in the world and demonstrated that there is an *infra-linear* correlation between growth and the cost of investment (it is more viable to build an extra kilometer of infrastructure than to build a new city) and a *supra-linear* correlation between these costs and the resulting externalities. This law explains why cities left to their own natural motion will extend like oil-slicks without anything being able to prevent this growth. It is positive externalities, but also, and increasingly, negative ones: pollution, crime, transport time, etc.

– Lastly **Zipf's law** states that the bigger the cities get, the fewer there are. In other words, larger cities absorb smaller ones to form megacities, with all of the side effects that come with them, such as an increase in inequalities, suburbanization, increased transport time, etc. In the USA since 1950, for every two growing urban centers, three have shrunk and 59 cities of over 100,000 residents have lost over 10% of their population.

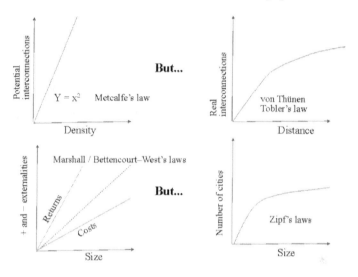

Figure 4.3. *The integration of laws of urban development*

Considering this, the ideal strategy, and one that Chinese planners are currently attempting, is to create clusters of medium-sized cities. The works of historian and anthropologist Joseph Tainter have demonstrated that the collapses of ancient (and modern!) empires were linked to their ability to control the complexity they had created. An increase in complexity is the foundation of a city's dynamic, **but complexity reaches a point where it is no longer governable and the system becomes turbulent**. Tainter observed that the only solution was then to reduce the surface of the system, something we saw in the case of the city of Detroit in the United States, which was a perfect example of a monotown.

From his ethnological analysis of the cities of ancient empires, Tainter [TAI 88] found a principle of the laws of complexity. If we let the elements in the system cumulate and connect to one another, complexity increases, and because it has not been designed, it becomes un-governable in application of Ashby's law. Typically, this is what happens with globalization where, ideologically, everything has been left to interconnect with everything, in particular in the financial field, which creates a non-governable turbulent system at the origin of crises. Tainter considers that this is what happened with ancient civilizations that disappeared: the unchecked growth of these empires allowed an ungovernable complexity to prosper. The only solution was then to collapse when complexity devoured the whole system, or simply to return to a governable size, which is what happened to modern and ancient empires.

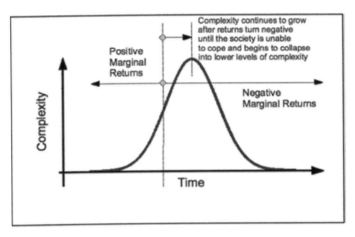

Figure 4.4. *From good to bad complexity, according to Joseph Tainter [TAI 88]*

For a city to create synergies, it needs complexity, good complexity, that is, governable complexity that produces positive marginal returns. However, beyond a certain point, these marginal returns become negative.

In the case of a city, recent analyses outline a critical G^* point, where the city produces optimal social benefits. Beyond that the city's marginal gains begin to decrease and it becomes preferable to build a new city rather than letting the city extend indefinitely when its complexity enters a zone of decreasing returns, meaning when the social benefit of the city in relation to its cost begins to decrease. There is a maximum size we will call G_{max} beyond which a city becomes a turbulent system, the cost of which outweighs its social benefits (Figure 4.5).

4.2.3. *What is a city's optimal size?*

How can we determine this point G*, and thus what is the optimal size of a city beyond which it will generate more negative externalities than positive ones? During his research on the subject, economic historian Paul Bairoch [BAI 77] looked at the necessary size to allow an industry to have the requisite synergies, starting from the critical size of a business during the second industrial revolution, based on mass production, and evaluated the minimum size for a city to be creating synergies to be 80,000 residents, its optimal size G* to be 300,000 people for an industrialized country, and the maximum size G_{max} to be 500,000, and a little more for non-industrialized countries. His calculation proceeded from an empirical analysis and not deductive research on the size of a city. The logics for searching for synergies at this time relied on the spatial concentrations on a same territory. Today, the size of industrial establishments has decreased – in particular with the outsourcing of production centers to low-salary countries – and they are connected to create virtual cooperative territories, which are the condition for economic synergies, but they do not create pockets of life.

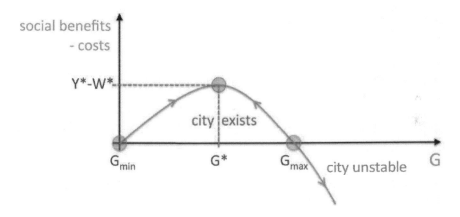

Figure 4.5. *The optimal size of a city. Source:*
L. Bettencourt The Origins of Scaling in Cities

The work of Paul Bairoch has not been reproduced to this day, but we can infer that in the new context of the *i*conomy creative cities can be smaller. This can be observed in France. In 2017, for the first time since the economic crisis in 2008, the country has opened more factories than it has shut down[3]. Those that were shut down appeared outside of cities and are the result of new, heavily automated processes. The *i*conomy tends to erase the difference between *manufacturing* and service activities: the latter cannot exist without the industrial basis of the former.

Mathematically, we can define the golden number of 1,500 people as the size of a group where everyone can be in interaction. At 20,000 people, everyone has a chance to interact, but beyond that, the possibility for interactions decreases. In a larger city, we can be totally isolated, crammed into transportation, communicate with no one... waiting to get home and get back to our "friends" on Facebook. Jane Jacobs, in her total critique of American urbanism [JAC 69], pleaded for cities to be structured as villages where everyone can encounter everyone.

4.2.4. *Size and inequalities are correlated*

Urban growth is out of control and correlated with a high growth in inequality and violence, which are products of social degradation. Urban growth is associated with a growth model linked to financial globalization, which moves urban industrial employment towards the service industry where inequalities in revenue increase[4]. This inequality translates geographically to the concentration of rich and poor into separate spaces, an increase in inequality which in the medium-term correlates with a break in development [OST 14] and in the long-term with urban violence and social unrest. In the USA, over the last 35 years, the gap between the richest 5% and the poorest 20% has increased considerably, and inequality is more profound and grows faster in large cities than in others (Figure 4.6).

This is a global tendency in both developed and developing countries. In wealthy countries, this is a result of policies that have favored the rich in the name of trickle-down economics[5]. In countries that are in the process of industrialization, this happens according to the principle of the Kuznets

3 See the trend analysis on Trendeo.fr.

4 See the report by Saskia Sassen [SAS 12].

5 The theory of trickle-down economics states that wealth will "trickle down" towards the middle class, even though they do not exist in poor countries, and that this effect will make the poor richer. This has never been successfully verified empirically.

curve[6]. In cities, inequality is cumulative: youth from the bottom echelons have a lower chance of accessing a quality education and find themselves trapped in a cycle of inequality. This inequality has begun to impede development [CIN 14]. The transition from one industrialization model to another – from the second to the third industrial revolution – translates into a process of *creative destruction* as identified by Joseph Schumpeter[7]: old jobs and qualifications disappear and their holders retreat to the outskirts of a city. The city then goes through a gentrification process, where the location of these neighborhoods becomes, in turn, a factor for exclusion.

Income growth for families at the 20th, 50th, and 95th percentiles, 1947–2013

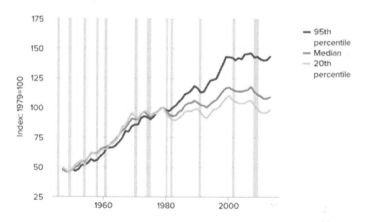

Figure 4.6. *Increasing inequality in large US cities. Data are for money income. Shaded areas denote recessions. (Source: [WIL 17], Tables F-1 and F-5)*

6 The principle of a Kuznets curve is an empirical observation formulated in 1955 according to which inequality increases in the early stages of development and decreases under the effect of redistributive policies. It is an observation and not a law, which would assume that this phenomenon is inevitable. Kuznets extended it to the environment, as countries became sensitive to environmental issues only past a certain point in their development. This principle currently needs to be refined slightly considering the evolution of sources of pollution and their outsourcing to developing countries by wealthy countries.

7 The principle of creative destruction as it was formulated by Schumpeter has nothing to do with its interpretation by neo-liberals who see it as a phenomenon of social Darwinism. When Schumpeter formulated this theory, it was in application to technologies, not businesses and even less so to individuals. The former have manifested surprising abilities in terms of resilience by reinventing their business models and production systems, while others failed and disappeared. We will see that the dynamism of social capital allows spectacular reconversions and that creative destruction in no way means "woe to the vanquished".

Inequality, unchecked growth, instability and loss of diversity – beyond the point G_{max} – are therefore linked. When making the case for diversity as fodder for creativity with a diverse population of families, entrepreneurs, artists, newcomers, old people and students, Jane Jacobs highlighted the fact that everyone could benefit this way from encountering all sorts of talent. In a city designed like this, everyone has a possibility of meeting everyone else in the street, which is an opportunity for innovation as opposed to a place of stress and insecurity. The way space is organized plays a role in the creation of synergies between the functions of the city by mixing all types of buildings (old houses, new buildings, offices, shops, churches, pubs and restaurants), and creating the possibility for things to happen at any moment and that these "new combinations" – which are the basis for innovation – occur.

Danish urbanist Jan Gehl [GEH 13] imagines the city from the point of view of a pedestrian moving 5 km/h. For him, the ideal city is Venice, with its multiple squares and alleys where people walk around, which encourages interactions. The counter-example is Brasilia, built by Oscar Niemeyer on the principles of Le Corbusier, where space is designed towards the magnificence of power and not for its residents. Gehl used his experience to develop five principles of urban architecture [BUD 16]: first, do not design a city necessitating automotive use because this forces residents to spend long hours at a stand-still in their cars, which has negative health effects. A study performed by *The Lancet* showed that a suburban resident's life-expectancy was decreased in correlation with their time spent in a car [SAL 16].

Next, public life must be based in the city. *"We should be walking more, spending more time in public spaces; we need to get out from our private spheres more often"* insists Gehl, which supposes a city built for pedestrians, which helps multiply sensations and experiences. This pedestrian experience must be amplified by equitable transports, like in Medellín, Columbia where the creation of transport networks with cable cars de-isolated the working-class areas at the height of the city, a place once controlled by the drugs and the cartels. Finally, cars are no longer a solution for urban transport, as demonstrated by the example of Singapore. There, they rolled out measures to keep cars off the road and made the cost of owning a car prohibitively expensive, coupled with effective public transport services, biking, and walking options.

This concept of the city is the exact opposite of the supposedly creative classes of Richard Florida whose creativity and dog spas is but an illusion and reinforces homogeneity in populations secluded to their areas.

4.3. Smart city: an autopoietic system

The internal coherence of a smart city brings us back to the principle of **organic growth** as identified in the medieval city. Christopher Alexander introduced the organic growth principle into the science of complex systems. An anthropologist and architect, Alexander wrote what is to this day one of the most successful books on urbanism and system architecture in general: *A Pattern Language*. Alexander compiled a toolkit of urban configurations (*patterns,* as he calls them) that can present the responses provided by the past to city-design. Alexander's fundamental idea is that the vast majority of questions asked today have been asked in the past, so he found answers that can be useful to us now. An architect's work can be assisted using this bank of solutions, by not reinventing them and rather focusing on how to *integrate* them, which is where the real innovation can be found[8]. Kind of like with Lego or blocks, all base elements are standardized and the architect's work is therefore to assemble all of these basic configurations to build shapes that will each be different. For example, Alexander wanted to fight the negative effects of work–home separation and defined the generic rules for "work distribution" (Figure 4.7).

---

8 Alexander's ideas found their application in the development of software system architecture such as designing integrated management software suites, which are built using the practices demonstrated in his book. This application shows us that the creative work is in the integration of these tools – or processes – with regard to a specific situation and not in copying them.

What are the requirements for a distribution of work that can overcome these problems?

1. Every home is within 20–30 minutes of many hundreds of workplaces.
2. Many workplaces are within walking distance of children and families.
3. Workers can go home casually for lunch, run errands, work half-time, and spend half the day at home.
4. Some workplaces are in homes; there are many opportunities for people to work from their homes or to take work home.
5. Neighborhoods are protected from the traffic and noise generated by "noxious" workplaces.

Figure 4.7. *Example of one of Alexander's patterns: configuration to help reduce distance from home to work*

In his first book, *A Timeless Way of Building*, Alexander describes organic growth as a system that organizes automatically where "the quality in buildings and in towns cannot be made, but only generated indirectly, by the ordinary actions of the people, just as a flower cannot be made, but only generated from the seed" [ALE 79]. We are therefore in the presence of what the Chilean researcher Humberto Maturana once called the autopoiesis of systems, or: "a network of processes of production (transformation and destruction) of components which: (1) through their interactions and transformations continuously regenerate and realize the network of processes that produced them; and (2) constitute it as a concrete unity in space in which they (the components) exist by specifying the topological domain of its realization as such a network". **The system produces and reproduces by integrating both internal (components) and external (environment) changes.**

We previously discussed how cities grow hierarchically, with neighborhoods absorbing others. However, that hierarchy is not – and must not be – rigid. In Alexander's mind, "a city is not a tree" [ALE 16] where everything is organized from the center that sucks its vitality from its surrounding. On the contrary, a "semilattice", a mesh that has a center which drives the city, organizes the zones to remain in interaction with one another.

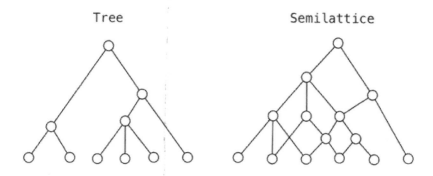

Figure 4.8. *The lattice architecture of a city (Christopher Alexander [ALE 16])*

Alexander considered that, instead of building physical connections because they are rational and neat, we needed to build physical connections where social connections are necessary. A city must be aligned with real-life and not the other way around, whereas "If we make cities which are trees, they will cut our life within to pieces". Alexander insists that functions should overlap in a physical space, unlike Le Corbusier's functionalism that was only capable of imagining play areas as dedicated spaces separate from anything else. In real life, activities overlap: if a city is structured around great communications axes, like Russian cities are, taxis still need to be able to stop when hailed by customers, and not disregard pedestrians.

Such an approach is therefore the exact opposite of the top-down design, the mass production approach that prevailed during the second industrial revolution. The similarity in approaches between France at that time and the Soviet Union is striking. During the post-war reconstruction, in the face of urgent need for housing, France simply stacked blocks (Figure 4.9).

For France this goes back even further with "Paris et le désert français" (Paris and the French Desert), according to the book by geographer Jean-François Gravier [GRA 47], which criticizes the exclusively central role of the city of Paris, and which went on to inspire the balancing policies of the French *Délégation à l'aménagement du territoire et à l'action Régionale* (DATAR; in English, Delegation of Land Planning and Regional Attractiveness).

Figure 4.9. *Monofunctional urbanization during the Krushchev era in Soviet Russia. Similarly to the great buildings in France, there was only one consideration in mind, the need for housing. These temporary habitations were designed to last 25 years at best; they are now having to be rebuilt (Photo by the author, Museum of the City of Moscow). For a color version of this figure, see www.iste.co.uk/rochet/cities.zip*

Urbanist Fabien Bellat performed a detailed study of the construction of Togliatti, a city built from scratch around a single purpose: automotive manufacturing. This type of city, which fits into the same architectural tradition as Le Corbusier and Oscar Niemeyer, served to express the power of an absolute central authority. They were not unaesthetic, nor were the buildings from the Baroque era, but they did not aim to build a city designed for its residents. They proceeded with a notion of ideal order designed from above to structure people's lives. Le Corbusier was a fascist militant in the 1920s and published his Athens Charter under the Vichy regime in 1943. This vision of urbanism was perfectly compatible with Stalinist urbanism. Le Corbusier also inspired the architect for Togliatti, Boris Roubanenko.

Figure 4.10. *Togliatti, an illustration of unique functionality, order and power. For a color version of this figure, see www.iste.co.uk/rochet/cities.zip*

The first time I presented my work in Russia, I was in front of a high-level and attentive auditorium, surprised by what was, for them, a novel approach. It was mentioned to me that there were smart cities under the USSR such as Akademgorodok. The approach was to populate the city with only smart and scientific people, something the USSR had in spades. However, this gave absurd results: a mass of intelligent people does not a smart city make. Everything depends on the creative interactions that the city will induce – or fail to do so – between them. In the time of the USSR, the approach, as it was in the Western world, was one of quantity: big is better. This is in fact still the *de facto* economic approach. The idea that the wealth, if not the intelligence, of a city should be the result of a systemic effect that would occur from an architecture that favors or does not favor creative synergies never crossed the minds of planners, or was instead considered to be some sort of *bourgeois* sophistication that was better off ignored.

On the opposite side of this school of thought, the **Aalborg Charter**[9] proposes a type of urbanism based on the principles of ecosystems that helps ensure urban sustainability by integrating industrial, political and environmental restrictions. This approach brings us closer to the principles of direct democracy and the need for cooperation between "all citizen partners, companies and interest groups" and by education in sustainability.

Figure 4.11. *Design thinking workshop in Christchurch. (Source: David Sim, Gehl Architects). For a color version of this figure, see www.iste.co.uk/rochet/cities.zip*

9 Adopted in 2004 by a consortium of European Cities, the Aalborg Charter opens the way to a new generation of less sectorial urban policies that attempt to integrate impacts on the environment on the short, medium and long term in an ecological and social dimension. This integration supposes the upset of five pillars of the Athens Charter:

(1) The decontextualization of architecture as a consequence of industrial standardization and the modern international style gives way to a concern for adapting to environments and an appreciation for local potentials. Inserting buildings into a city following ecological, landscape and cultural criteria are the characteristics of a "sustainable" architecture.

(2) The clean slate principle is argued against in the name of appreciation for smart heritage and territory.

(3) Zoning is replaced with a search for social and functional diversity, susceptible to slow down the growing need for mobility and the process of socio-spatial segregation.

(4) Extending the limits of the city as encouraged by Le Corbusier is discouraged in favor of containing urbanization, in order to halt the consumption of space, infrastructures and energy.

(5) Conversely to the type of urbanism preached by the rational experts of the 1930s, the Aalborg Charter defends a construction of the city that is open to participation.

A centralized top-down approach is replaced with an *emergence* of the city from the real lives of the people living inside it and conceiving their city as a *system of life*. One such experiment is currently ongoing in the city of **Christchurch**, the second largest city in New Zealand. Christchurch was destroyed by an earthquake in 2011, and the residents decided that for their city to be truly resilient and evolve, it had to be designed from the bottom-up based on the vision its residents have of their own system of life (Figure 4.11).

4.4. A city must be designed as a "system of systems"

The **smart city** as a system calls for radical scientific and industrial breakthroughs, which will require a new way of modeling and thinking about complexity. If we hypothesize that a sustainable city is a smart city able to learn thanks to the feedback loops it creates with its environment, it behaves as an ecosystem and is therefore capable of evolving its own rules by itself. In systems science and in institutional economics, this is called an *auto-regulatory system*, which supposes that at its core it has a *genetic* code the same way a natural system does. New approaches in complex systems architecture such as biomimicry[10] show that through a long process of trial and error (3.8 billion years of R&D, according to Janine Benyus), nature was able to design systems both resilient and complex based on a single renewable energy: the Sun.

In the *i*conomy, the power of computers, the mass of data they can process, and the development of programming languages that can allow us to model cities as systems of systems can create this code, where classic public management had to make do with managing a couple of loosely connected functions (housing, work, infrastructures, energy… with as many separate policies) while being forced to play catch-up with negative effects induced by modeling errors while even globalization continuously creates uncontrolled complexity.

The history of economic development teaches us that the endogenous dynamic of human systems are able to create, in time, auto-reinforcing institutions, but that that does not exclude the intervention of an exogenous actor setting the rules of the game – the institutions – appropriate to development, that is, the State. This dynamic is always present in the *i*conomy, but it mobilizes a number of parameters and does so much faster.

---

10 Biomimicry was analyzed by Janine Benyus.

Where the retroactions between causes and effects that enable learning used to take at least a generation, they can now occur within a millisecond.

The idea is not to let urban systems develop around digital technologies, thus granting the masters of said technology complete control[11]. The age-old question of institutional economics can be asked: "Who will regulate the regulators?"

This highlights the importance for states to develop architectural abilities for systems of systems, which we include in the notion of ULM – *urban lifecycle management*. Instead of thinking of technology as *exogenous* to development by the accumulation of technological components on the surface of a dysfunctional urban fabric, the idea is to think of technology as an *endogenous* lever of transformation. While emerging countries, China and India among them, are beginning to think of a city as a global integrated system, Westerners continue to think of a city as a sum of technical systems for which they have a commercial supply, even when Western urban policies are overall failing in spite of recent improvements. Chinese urban strategy recognizes the mistake in imitating the West when Singapore is a success that is conceived as an ecosystem, a smart nation rather than a smart city, and is now a reference point for urban development.

These abilities will therefore have to allow us to confront two major issues: mastering the principles of innovation in the *i*conomy to design the code and allow its sustainability by granting it systemic "eco" properties by its own operation ensured by the very life of the city:

– A city is not smart because it is digital: the connection of everything to everything, the intrusive ability of mass data processing and their threat to confidentiality can quickly pull a city towards Jeremy Bentham's *panopticon*[12]. An integrative vision of smart cities tends to establish itself

---

11 GAFA (Google, Facebook, Apple, Amazon), all American firms, weigh more than France's CAC40.

12 In 1786, British philosopher Jeremy Bentham (1748–1832) imagined a new architectural form which would put an end to the scandal of filth and dirt in prisons: the panopticon in its design guaranteed generalized surveillance and helped organize the condition of the prisoner with an aim to make him or her profitable for society. This utilitarian obsession abandoned all ethics and embraced a totalitarian utopia. This idea of progress did manage to seduce certain members of the French Revolution since one French deputy presented the synthesis translated by Étienne Dumont to the assembly in 1791.

[GIL 15], which cannot be summarized as a sum of "smart services" – *smart grids, smart buildings, smart mobility, smart IT...* – but rather as a living ecosystem where the intelligence comes from the behavior of its citizens, making technology an endogenous lever for development of civic life by simultaneously making the citizens information producers and users, along the logic of web 2.0.

– Designing complex ecosystems cannot be ensured by top-down planning procedures by a public authority that defines "master plans" in which the father of contemporary system architecture, Christopher Alexander [ALE 77], saw the seeds of a totalitarian order incapable of organic evolution. The new approaches of innovation based on complex systems, in particular those developed by Eric von Hippel [VON 86], highlight the need to integrate the end-user, but also an information producer, that the literature refers to as a *prod-user*.

– Digital technology itself asks radically new questions and is *both a problem and a solution*. Let us take the case of calculators and data banks (*data centers*). Their power is the condition of performance of the connected city. However, this power dissipates, on the one hand, a considerable amount of energy and requires even more power to cool it down and, on the other hand, the fabrication of these machines consumes a lot of energy and water. Today, these data centers consume 10% of electricity in France. The goal is now to define machines that behave as "pro-sumers". Instead of using even more energy to cool down these machines, they must use their computing power to optimize their own supply of various sources of energy and integrate energy dissipation into a city's design for urban heating and climate control, for example. Many pilot sites do exist, but the balance is far from optimal[13].

– This genetic code of the smart city thusly designed will be nourished by the dynamic of auto-reinforcing institutions based on the lives of residents. Christchurch, New-Zealand, was destroyed in an earthquake in 2011, and we now see two approaches facing off: the government's, which has created a unique reconstruction agency in the name of efficiency, and the City Mayor's, who, on the contrary, sees integrating the residents' initiative into the design of the city as the best guarantee for resilience. The main source of discussion is the question of density: a more densely populated city encourages synergies and saves on power, whereas a more scattered city

---

13 The first positive energy data center was built in Falun, Sweden, in March 2016.

population gives everyone space [NEW 98], but encourages automotive use and thus energy consumption. This notion is now being disputed by the decrease in automotive consumption and the autonomous production of renewable energy, which is dependent on available space [MÉN 11].

The issue is mastering the notion of systems that will one day be capable of auto-regulation and controlling the complexity that rests on the integration of heterogeneous systems (that is, systems of systems).

Systems of systems (SoS) are systems that can be broken down into smaller independent systems that operate autonomously and follow their own evolution. The coherence of a SoS relies on coupling the evolutions of the systems within it. Yet, this coupling is "far from equilibrium", to use the expression from Michael Batty. A technical system can evolve and be decoupled from the other technical systems. For example, in Songdo, Korea, connectivity has been based on RFID chips, made obsolete by people's smartphones. The evolution of a system can stimulate innovation and evolution in another, but also block an evolution. We remember the mayors of Parthenay and Agde, France, who pioneered the installation of Internet in their towns and who were eliminated by their electors in 2001. One common reproach: the cost of technological sophistication was too great at the expense of real life. What is the point of being able to send an email that takes a couple of seconds to signal a dysfunction if the reaction from the technical services still takes as long? The technical system and the organizational system were decoupled, and the voters punished those responsible.

A technology is not a supplement that can be added to the surface of something to magically transform it. A technology is part of a technical system when it is more than just an isolated technique destined to perform automatisms. For example, when the first age of computing automated the production of payslips, it was only a question of performing previous manual tasks faster and more efficiently, without the payment process being affected.

Gilbert Simondon [SIM 12], who was the first great philosopher of technique during the era of information, introduced the notion of "coupling" in order to understand the technical object. Either a technical object is just an autonomous element that is not coupled with another element, or it is coupled with another element or human. This technical object can therefore not be understood without a global comprehension of the relation it maintains with humans. It is important to understand how each element of the couple operates and how they interact through the coupling. *The element alone cannot lead to overall understanding.*

Coupling is therefore a critical axis for an urban manager, who will have to ask themselves a few questions:

– What is the impact of an evolution in a system on another system, or even the SoS as a whole?

– How can we ensure the coupling between technical systems and human systems? The common discourse by technology vendors is to sell trainings for "change management". In other words, people must adapt to technology and they are naturally conservative, unintelligent and retrograde. As we will see, sustainable innovations actually come from people and not technology.

– How do boundaries of SoS evolve? For example, can a transport system change the connection between a city and its environment and therefore change the border of the city? For example, cities connected by the TGV to Paris see their population change when they are suddenly within an hour commute to Paris and see their position change from a city at the heart of their territory to a city on the outskirts of a different territory.

To answer these questions, we need a model – an abstract representation of reality – which shares the essential properties of the original but is much easier to manipulate and understand. Digital technologies help build this representation on computer and determine how these properties change through time and under the effect of internal and external events.

4.4.1. *Modeling*

As with any good system, the concept of sustainable urban ecosystem can be defined by its finality, or, in the case of an inhabited system, a *common good* that is superior to the sum of its parts, and the interactions between functions – which we analyze here, in the logic of systems of systems, as sub-systems – that are composed of: water, food, health, energy, urban and intercity transports, housing, work, digital economy, leisure, sports, etc.

The **principle of modeling** supposes that we can define, within a frame of reference encompassing the multiple visions of urban reality, variable *parameters* for all cities wherever they are, since all cities must manage transportation functions, energy, housing, etc., and integrate them. This is the value of these parameters (the *variables*), which will change according to context, parameters that will not be taken into account everywhere (for example, the "typhoon management" parameter will only be taken into account in known vulnerable areas) and cannot be enumerated definitively (the technological risk can outline new parameters). What is more, the interactions between these different functions of the system that generate uncontrolled *emergences*, that can only be so through an evolving and learning modeling effort that reinforces resilience.

This supposes that stakeholders have the *same information bases* and the *same rules for describing data* (semantic and syntax) to enter into integrative processes. In the field of building construction, the BIM standard (building information modeling) is a modeling language that allows project managers and overseers to integrate their projects into a 6D representation (three spatial dimensions, plus time, cost and maintenance through time). BIM has existed since 1987, when the first version of virtualization software ArchiCAD was released by Graphisoft. It allows users to manage the entire lifecycle of a building, from its design to its demolition, thus encouraging recycling (ecological footprint of materials, repurposing, etc.), and integrates perfectly into PLM logic (product lifecycle management).

BIM's underlying logic is one of system architecture: concentrating efforts on integration from the very beginning. The absence of integration will cause the data to be entered twice (it is estimated that the geometric data of a building are entered seven times in total during its building process) with the inherent multiplication of mistakes, and written in different programming languages and software. The downstream cost of these mistakes is, in France, estimated at approximately 10 billion euros. Through BIM, these chunks of information represented in a common standard become reusable *building blocks* for each job system thanks to a common exchange format IFC (industry foundation classes). Initially limited to actual buildings, this language extends to environmental impacts (*green BIM*). From central physical variables, modeling tools extend progressively to the environment of a project and help visualize the final impact of a hypothesis.

The BIM standard is a **public good** developed by clusters of companies, pushed by academic institutions including the University of Stanford. This language has become prevalent in Asian markets with increasing amounts of

Chinese graduates trained in its use. Use of the BIM standard is now mandatory in Singapore and will soon be in a number of other Asian countries.

This approach to modeling immediately removes the idea of a "green city" that would have zero carbon emissions or waste production, which could never be a complete city incorporating all urban activities as it would have to remove all carbon emissions and environmental impacts of imported activities.

Designing an urban ecosystem is first and foremost a problem of **global architecture of sub-systems** that it is composed of, as well as a problem of understanding and taking into account human behavioral factors. The research hypothesis, derived from complex systems architecture, is that it is possible to define a *reference framework*[14] of urban ecosystems, which will allow us to integrate these functions and will create a variety of models depending on the values attributed to the parameters. This framework defines the rule for how the building blocks will fit together, a common language for all activities, interfacing methods, databases and semantic processing rules.

Complex systems architecture then acts as an *integrative discipline*, reintroducing the possibility to control. From a vision that stacks specialized functions on top of one another, separated by their own specific technical logics and each one concerned with their own optimization, it offers an approach that incorporates interaction between the different functions. Therefore, *local optimization does not necessarily mean global optimization*: the over-optimization of some functions can result in an under-optimization of the overall system. The fascination we have at the moment with bicycles as the solution to urban pollution may result in said pollution is instead ejected out of the city; one iconic and pathological illustration of this being the case of Paris's municipal policy which has resulted in an increase in overall pollution around Paris, in exchange for a localized decrease in automotive emissions.

Each of these functions can be considered as a parameter for a governing variable that varies depending on the contexts between limit values given by

14 A framework is "a set of usable tools for developing a large range of architectures", in other words, a series of valid design rules and methods, within defined limitations, for all sustainable urban ecosystems. Not to be confused with a unique modeling tool that would encapsulate all individual cases, which, in practice, would be impossible.

environmental restrictions (for example, the maximum supply or water-processing capacity) or by the designer's impetus who will decide to limit the scale of the city to a given number of residents. Depending on the context, we will choose to control first the parameter of "energy", or of "water", etc.

It cannot be a generic model that makes it possible to design any city in any environment. The number of parameters and limit values they take on cannot be determined before the fact with any amount of certainty, for example, an arid area or a monsoon area, even if, in theory it is possible to rise in levels of abstractness and define the framework for the framework, as complexity grows, modeling activities is performed from the reality of a type of city and, in the medium term, will define these meta-rules through the multiplication of pilot projects.

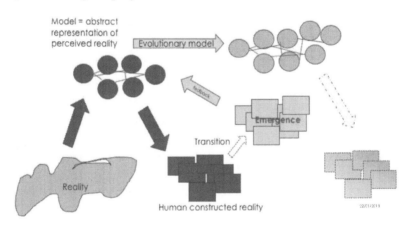

Figure 4.12. *Modeling as a dialog between reality and an objective*

In practice, *each ecosystem will be different,* since it will be the result of a compounding of these parameters that depend on the political, social and economic factors of different contexts. Modeling work is therefore a perpetually evolving dialog between an abstract representation of a reality and that reality itself, as shown in Figure 4.12. A reality is used to extract recurring elements which can be turned into sub-systems – transport, waste management, housing, civic life, leisure, etc. – to a sufficient level of abstraction for which they can be applied to all cities. A city planner then studies how for which they can organize this reality into the abstract. This is where modern digital tools will be of great use, enabling a user to load the parameters model, then the context-sensitive variables model onto a testing build to experiment with the pertinence of a model and then a scenario applied to said model. This scenario and model are then translated into reality by pilot projects, which serve to test real life solutions. Using successive feedback loops, the model will grow more and more precise and will incorporate *emergences*.

4.4.2. Emergence

A sailboat's navigator embarking upon a trip across the world will have planned for any of the great phenomena that they know could occur: storms, shipwreck, icebergs and undertow, and will manage his ship's complexity in consequence. The navigator will predict that these events *could* occur, but cannot forecast *when*, *where* or with *what magnitude*. In the systemic modeling process, all we have is the generic, *all specificity eludes us*. The final result is an *emergent* reality that will result of the random combination of various environmental factors. To effectively prepare for the trip, the navigator will identify behavioral models in his boat: how it reacts to various winds, to the sea, how it steers, etc. They will then build a framework of possible combinations of behavior and potential phenomena. This framework represents the rules of composition of different models. If the framework is not sufficiently complex, it will not be capable of predicting appropriate navigating behaviors. In addition, from one trip to another, the navigator knows they will never finish discovering new unpredicted phenomena. By definition, a framework, just like a model, is a limited representation of complex phenomena that it is supposed to describe. Upon returning from trips, the navigator will exchange experiences with other navigators in order to improve their framework, knowing all the while that it will always be desperately incomplete.

While at the macroscopic level, a framework is useful for predicting phenomena, at a microscopic level – day-to-day life of the ship – there will only be access to a limited number of models corresponding to the parts of the ship and its navigation systems. A navigator wishing to model all phenomena would expose themself to the Titanic syndrome: "there cannot be any icebergs and the ship is unsinkable", with the end that line of thinking implies. The navigator is the one who will be able to welcome novelty, randomness and invent appropriate responses, using a set of skills and evaluating the adequacy of their behavior thanks to the feedback that their environment provides.

An emergent phenomenon is the result of interactions of a number of sub-systems. In a car, for example, comfort is an emergent phenomenon. It is the product of an interaction between sub-systems "pleasant driving", "chassis" and "acoustics". These sub-systems are emergent in that they are the results of interactions between other sub-systems. As we saw in the example of the city of Marseille that "aging well in the city" is an emergence of heterogeneous phenomena and functions (Figure 4.16). Herbert A. Simon showed us that complex systems form a tree-branch structure, where the properties of a higher-tier system, the "global", can be reduced to those of lower-tier systems, the "parts". The overall system then in turn becomes a higher-echelon emergent system.

In a car, one of the most complex industrial products, the "comfort" system is an emergent property in modern vehicles in that it does not correspond to a basic sub-system. This is all the more true in a city that will integrate conservative and adaptive systems. Governing emergence will begin by defining the perimeter of sub-systems that enter into play, such "aging well in the city". However, we can never claim to have exhaustively catalogued all sub-systems that influence aging well. All the more so that sub-systems themselves are emergent phenomena (for example, the sub-system "housing"). Mapping these emergent relations is all the more complex since one sub-system can contribute to the emergence of numerous systems: we can model some of these phenomena but we can never be sure that this model is complete. To make this model legible, the designer must focus on the most important interactions, knowing that emergence cannot entirely obey the goals we set it. There is always a portion of randomness, or at the very least blindness, which will encounter a principle of **auto-organization**. Auto-organization is a process of organization of a set of moving parts that occurs automatically. Incrementally, we are able to define coherent configurations, always far from the equilibrium, and relatively controllable, but it will never be possible to say that we have reached the summit of the tree structure and thus neutralized the possibility for emergences. *All progress in the mastery of stable complex systems creates long-term systems emergences that are even more complex and un-mastered.*

Modeling is therefore a continuous process that is part of city governance, and is just like any complex system that always holds unexpected emergences, which will question established models.

4.4.3. *Evolution inside: the urban lifecycle management*

Since the "death of distance" with the revolution of transport methods in the middle of the 19th Century, we have seen the appearance of transport, telecommunications networks, the telegraph, etc., all of which have transformed the administration of the city and removed obstacles to a cities' growth. Today, information technologies and globalization mark a new "death of distance" and amplify this movement with new tools such as smartphones that have become the Swiss army knives of the smart city allowing residents to be stakeholders in the city coordinating and communicating, feeding the big data machines. In doing so, digital technologies can produce the best and the worst. Each city contains the components that could cause its own destruction: the rapid propagation of information amplifies all social phenomena, makes inequalities more pronounced, opens the door to strategies of destabilization and intoxication, even thought control: universal communication does not necessarily tend towards truth, but can lead to a vision of the city reminiscent of Orwell's Big Brother controlling people's language and minds. As a system far from equilibrium, a city is continuously subject to forces of decomposition making it important to control its evolution.

The sustainability of these ecosystems rests on their **abilities to evolve** depending on the variation of internal and external parameters: lifecycles depending on their parts, exogenous technological changes and **absorptive capacity**[15] of firms. In this perspective, the ecosystem is capable of learning, accounting for the path dependency phenomenon[16] (or technological

---

15 The *ability for absorption* is a fundamental concept in economics intelligence: this is the ability to recognize the value of information, new idea or scientific progress, to transform into an economic opportunity. North American firms that have outsourced their R&D to emerging countries control this indicator to measure if it is still possible to transform advances performed in foreign countries faster.

16 Path dependency is the result of a chain of cumulative causalities, each effect becoming more dependent on the causal chain. The more we learn, the more we can learn, but more we are conditioned by this way of learning and what we already know. Individuals and

trajectory) identified by evolutionist economists, which involves evaluating the ecosystem's history and the dynamic of its social capital. Eric von Hippel's research shows that knowledge is sticky and very hard to move from one territory to another.

As with any system, an ecosystem tends towards homeostasis, meaning identical reproduction with the ability to evolve along a technological trajectory. This is both an advantage, since the territory is constitutive of its competitive advantage (it can neither be copied nor moved), and an inconvenience in case of a technological split that requires trajectory tuning.

As a system of systems, the urban ecosystem includes two types of regulatory systems:

– On the one hand, flow regulation systems can be modeled according to the laws of physics – these are known as **conservative systems** – such as *smart grids* for electricity, but the principle of which also applies to water (*smart water*), the performance of which depends directly on the digital systems that catch and process data and send appropriate instructions.

– On the other hand, qualitative systems – known as **dissipative systems** – are based on essentially organizational and human interactions that can be explained only by the principles of sociology or institutional economics.

Therefore the system "health in the city" will be the emergence of a system reflecting the type of social life that allows residents to live healthily (for example, keeping elderly people in a socially rich and rewarding environment) and a physical system composed of health centers spanning pharmacies to big hospitals.

The issue will be in the ability to design systems focused on specific parameters: carbon-free energies in developed countries, water processing, management and distribution systems, and then complete urban ecosystems like clean cities, for example. China, after seeing the results of the city of Dongtan has recently collaborated with British firm Arup to order an ecocity based on the integration of city and countryside in Wanzhuang that would in

---

organizations become less and less receptive to external ideas and lose their ability to innovate, which explains how great firm leaders get outplayed by outsiders.

effect be a cluster of cutting-edge traditional rural economic activities. The goal is to design an integrated development of Chinese traditional rural activities with industrial ones in the context of a medium-sized city of 400,000 residents.

4.4.4. *System architecture as a frame of representation*

Architecture offers a **conceptual framework** to integrate these sub-systems in order to design a system that can be regulated[17]. The systemic architecture's design presents a number of problems:

– A system cannot be integrated by the sum of its sub-systems: the system possesses **emergent properties**, which cannot be modeled in sub-systems and are the product of interactions between them. Typically, functions of "security" or "comfort" in a vehicle cannot be tied to any one particular system, but are an emergent property. An energy-plus-city with positive energy is not the sum of energy-plus-buildings. A system is structured by interactions between its functions in service of a single goal: common good.

– The **common good of a system** is an emergent function that needs to be controlled. Garett Hardin illustrated this problem in *The Tragedy of the Commons* [HAR 68]: if each shepherd optimizes the use of commons to improve its productivity, they decrease overall productivity and destroy the common good. Elinor Ostrom [OST 91] showed that, conversely, communities were able to *create institutions* to avoid the tragedy of the common. Understanding emergences is therefore at the core of the modeling process.

– The **functional vision** is an abstract representation of what this system must do, a model ("we reason exclusively in models", says Paul Valéry) for which we must first define the outlines (a system is always the sub-system of a larger system) depending on the finality we wish to achieve with it and the ability to govern it.

---

17 A system that can be regulated is a system for which we can determine the control parameters using information feedback. The opposite of a system that can be regulated is a chaotic system, which is a semi-deterministic system where we cannot completely comprehend the laws governing its behavior.

The **complexity** of the model is a function of the number of interactions between its components. This complexity is increased by the *misalignment of three reference points*: the "operations" are performed by "functions" that can serve more than one operation, and are served by "organs" that serve more than one function, according to the diagram by Daniel Krob (Figure 4.6).

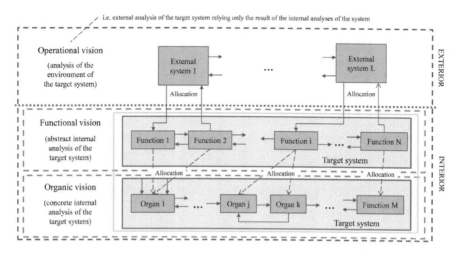

Figure 4.13. *Generic diagram of system integration. (Source: Daniel Krob)*

We can see that the issue of integration is a delicate art which, on the one hand, will have to adopt the right level of abstraction of the target model, identify the desirable and undesirable interactions, and, on the other hand, look for the maximum interoperability of functions and organs. The idea is therefore to define a pertinent level of complexity that unites three qualities: the ability to complete a task, controllability and economy.

System architecture helps respond to the contradiction between the idea of making a perfect city and, on the other hand, the total absence of any frame of reference. Christopher Alexander, the anthropologist and architect, wrote a book which, to this day, remains one of the most successful books on urbanism, *A Pattern Language*. Alexander compiled a toolkit of urban configurations (*patterns*, as he calls them) that can present responses provided by the past to city design. Alexander's fundamental idea is that the great majority of questions asked in the past are still relevant today. A pattern is a stable and reusable configuration, made of physical elements that have relations with their environment and which solve a problem by integrating all restrictions without conflict. The work of the architect can therefore be assisted using this database of solutions, without reinventing them and focusing on integration, which is where real innovation occurs. For example, to fight against the negative effects of the separation between housing and workplace, Alexander defines generic rules on "distributed work" (see Figure 4.7).

4.4.5. *The design method*

The city has a finality that is a strategic vision held by stakeholders, public authorities, industrial operators and residents who will bring life to this system through their interactions with one another and their environment.

This finality deploys in an arborescence of functions, which determine what the city *must* do to complete its task. These functions fit into *soft* fields (human systems such as education, well-being, leisure, work and civic life) and other *hard* fields (physical systems such as energy, transportation, housing and waste management). What make a city smart and resilient are the connections between the various branches. We are talking here of arborescence in the sense of the arborescence of complex systems as defined by Herbert A. Simon [SIM 96], where the designer connects sub-systems in order to favor an emergence corresponding to a specific goal. This is the opposite of the approach criticized by Christopher Alexander in his commentary *A City is Not a Tree* as part of his analysis of the *urban planning* movement in the USA, which did not plan for any connections between branches, something Alexander described as "a fight against complexity". Modern cities designed for cars offer few connections. This idea of considering the whole thing as a modular combination of reusable patterns has for a long time remained foreign to architects, but has been widely accepted in another field of complex systems engineering: SOA (service-oriented architecture).

These functions require tools, artifacts, specialized workers and ordinary citizens. The critical point is that when *solutionists* tell ordinary people to adapt to their tools (a great opportunity for businesses to sell a "change management" contract), it is actually the tools that need to adapt to their users. The case we present further down on eco-conception of a supply system of drinking water is remarkable in that it mobilizes indigenous knowledge systems in areas where importing sophisticated foreign technologies have failed in the past.

The city as an ecosystem can be represented by Figure 4.14:

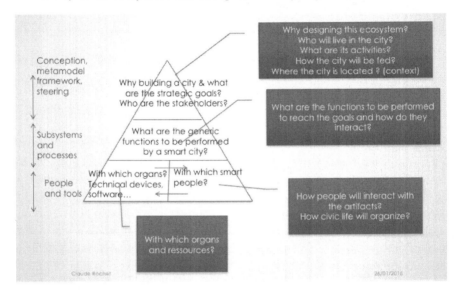

Figure 4.14. *A representation of a city as an ecosystem*

Daniel Krob[18], founder of this "triangular" modeling approach, considers that modeling an ecosystem supposes a response to three questions:

– The first is *why* a city, what is its reason for existing and what are its goals in terms of *who* its stakeholders are and *what* activities it wishes to host. Asking these questions – and keeping them in mind – is crucial to avoid drifting to a technocentric approach to cities, which relies on techno-determinism, as we saw in Chapter 1.

---

18 Daniel Krob is the founder of the CESAMES which provides training in complex systems structures [KRO 09].

– The second is *what.* What are the functions that a city must provide to meet its objectives. They will help define processes that can be grouped into sub-systems.

– The third question is *how.* How will these functions operate with technical organs managed by specialist workers, with business and city executives, in interaction with the city's end users (residents).

Once again, the idea is not to design a model of a perfect city where every requisite interaction is perfectly adjusted, but rather to define the *modeling rules* that will be able to accompany a city's development and evolution throughout its lifecycle, a model that can constantly update itself depending on the results it obtains and the problems encountered by the city in question. The quality of these rules will determine a city's sustainability.

4.4.5.1. *Lifecycle management*

Products have an evolution that spans from their design to their death. PLM (product lifecycle management) was invented to govern this lifecycle by coordinating all the involved operators and their inputs. PLM links all of the operators involved in designing the product (marketing, sales, clients, case studies, fabrication, logistics, contractors, services, maintenance, recycling, etc.). Its advantage is that it allows an industry to accelerate and optimize the design phases, anticipate validations and simulations without having to proceed to fabrication thanks to complete situational virtual modeling, to remove any approximations, to link and automate all industrial processes, integrate the product and the services that are associated with it, to reduce production costs and deadlines. In practice, it defines meta-rules, a meta-product, the same way we can define the meta-rules of a city.

The difference is that a city, unlike a product, does not die; it constantly evolves. To this end, the *Urban Lifecycle Management©* (ULM) [ROC 16a] was developed. A non-smart city will continuously increase according to the law established by Geoffrey West and Luis Bettencourt. Complexity then gets out of control: the city becomes a sum of heterogeneous neighborhoods with high social and spatial inequalities.

ULM (Figure 4.15) is a design tool oriented towards coherent ecosystems with the political, social and economic goals of a sustainable city:

low-energy footprint, waste recycling and managed growth, in order to plan its evolution and control its transition through the ages. ULM must counteract the appeal of techno-determinism by governing the entire lifecycle of the city using the following considerations:

– A city cannot be designed in isolation from its territorial or historical context. As we will see further down, cities that develop in unlikely places *always* have a history. In addition, it must be developed from a strategic analysis of its context, its history and its assets, in interaction with its territory according to the principles we discussed earlier of *smart territory*.

– To be a living city, it cannot be a prototype the way Masdar, Unitied Arab Emirates, is. On the contrary, the designer will focus on integrating systems, tools, and "off the shelf" solutions, meaning ones that have already had a social or industrial life like Christopher Alexander's patterns. It is an extension of the idea that "you can't reinvent the brick if you're reinventing the house" if we want to design a sustainable city. This will require a coordination of innovation cycles of the components of the city, which have different rhythms and crossed impacts which will need to be modeled in order to anticipate them.

– In the case of a new city, the process described in Figure 4.9 leads to a first version of the city through a governance course of complex projects such as the ones modeled by Roger Miller [MIL 00]. At this point, similarly to the case of an existing city, we need to understand how a city lives and evolves. There will always be a gap between the designer's intention and the end result; the city would therefore need an observatory of sorts to collect data on the city. This is where Big Data will become very useful, especially with data produced from smartphones, the Swiss-army knife of the smart city, which has the advantage of equipping the cities of emerging countries where informal housing is very prominent.

– Throughout this lifecycle, exogenous innovations arise (new technologies, new materials, etc.), which must be integrated into the model. Songdo, in Korea, for example, was designed in 2004 to collect data from RFID chips, which became obsolete with the rise of smartphones[19].

---

19 The first smartphone was invented by IBM in 1993, it became a mass-market product in 2007 with Apple's famous iPhone.

Innovation in connected automobiles will interact with urban transport systems – physical conservative systems – and with the behavior of conductors – human dissipative systems. A common frame of coordination for these evolutions will be necessary, a tool and a role that still remain to be created.

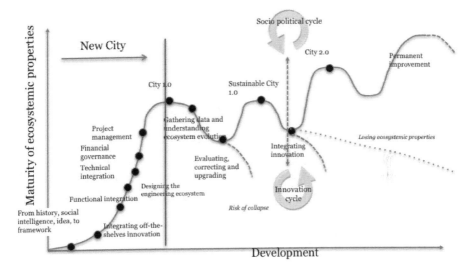

Figure 4.15. *Urban Lifecycle Management© Claude Rochet*

– Innovation continuously tests a city's equilibrium. All of these are neither good nor desirable, hence the importance of managing the tension between the evolution of civic life and the evolution of technology. Change is not inherently good, unlike many modern tendencies suggest. Does it serve the greater good or not? The development of electronic systems can prove to be intrusive and impact collective and individual liberties. There are innovations which we must refuse.

– Throughout its evolution, a city will tend to lose its intelligence, which will have two undesirable consequences: it can begin to expand in an oil-slick pattern under the effect of imbalances between the city and its territory, of an increase in rural exodus or population migrations. If its core activity begins to decline, it will have to undertake a reconversion or suffer the fate of monotowns. It can become a megalopolis, a conurbation too complex to be controlled, something that was demonstrated by Joseph

Tainter[20]. Its size will have to be reduced – something that happened in Detroit – or it will have to follow the long, hard road towards reindustrialization like the Russian monotowns did.

4.4.6. *Integration process: more efficiency for less*

No two cities are identical, but according to the principles of system architecture as they are understood by ULM, common rules can be defined. One of these rules concerns the interactions between economic development and human capital. For a city to be attractive, it must have strong infrastructures while not being too big to be able to guarantee a good quality of life. We have seen the illusion, the impasse and the negative consequences of policies aimed towards the "creative classes" inspired by Richard Florida.

Innovation cannot be imported as it is always a product of the environment, the social capital and the territory. No matter the level of this initial social capital, growth must come from its ability to appropriate technologies as we will see in the example of the Moroccan experiment e-douar. There is a cycle of positive reinforcement between the increase in the number of end-users of a given technology, pertinent technological development and the quality of urban life. All the more so that, in a digital city, the end-user also becomes a *prod-user*, according to the concept created by sociologist Axel Burns. This prod-user will be an operator of the ongoing process of innovation, which becomes increasingly more endogenous as the city and its social capital develop. This is the condition to avoid a technological fracture from appearing between the connected and the disconnected.

Modeling rules must follow these three principles:

1) **Strategic analysis**: The first task is to define the issues of the city with the stakeholders: What are the issues? What are the city's goals? How do people want to live there? What are the inevitable restrictions linked, for example, to the physical environment, climate, accessibility and finality: we can stipulate that each neighborhood be a 20,000-person entity to allow its residents to meet, set a maximum size for buildings and define traffic and parking laws, etc.

---

20 See Figure 4.4.

2) **Catalog all building blocks**. There are essential elements due to necessity – risk of flooding, seismic area, extreme climate, etc. – but also depending on desired synergies (not only internal ones), and with regard to traffic flow and international commerce. On this level, it is important to integrate elements that are not necessarily required just yet, such as due to climate change, for example, extreme cold, rising sea-levels, flooding, etc.

This connects with Christopher Alexander's patterns. Designing a city is like playing with Lego. Depending on the problem at hand, it is important to catalog the building blocks that will be needed. Figure 4.10 represents the operation: the column on the left lists problems that may be encountered. This is a non-exhaustive list and would require perfecting depending on the context of the city. These questions are linked to a function of the city (the second level of the triangle in Figure 4.6) and define the resources to employ in the third column. The fourth column lists the processes and abilities to employ to process these questions.

Issues	Functions	Resources	Capabilities
• Defining "smartness" and "sustainability"	• Work	• Energy	• The New Business Models:
• Wealth creation	• Budgeting	• Water	• Public
• Finance and taxes	• Transportation	• Data	• Private
• Controlling pollution	• Feeding	• Digital systems	• Project management
• Equilibrium center – periphery	• Caring	• Traditions	• Institutional arrangements
• Migrations	• Protecting	• Sociology	• The day to day decision-making process in an evolutionary perspective
• Poverty	• Securing	• Technologies as enablers and enacters	• Empowerment
• Education	• Housing policy	• Culture and traditions	• Direct democracy
• Health	• Education	• Institutions and public organizations	• Government

• Crime	• Leisure	• Process modeling	• Governance
• Segregation (social and spatial)	• Social benefits	• Software	• Project management
• Leisure	• Health care system	• Tech providers	• Social innovation
• Quality of life	• Migrations control	• Open innovation	• The state as a system engineer
• How do people interact with people and artifacts?			• Mastering ULM

Table 4.1. *Building blocks*

In line with Christoper Alexander's patterns, American architects Andres Duany and Jeff Speck catalogued 148 principles of urban architecture in "The smart growth manual" [DUA 11], the principles of which are presented at http://smartgrowth.org.

3) **Integrating the ecosystem**. We have seen that in systems dynamics, a system's behavior is an emergence, meaning that it cannot be attributed to a single element, function or sub-system. More often than not, the over-optimization of a single element will result in a sub-optimization of the overarching system. This is the case when one solution is granted too great a focus, like the bicycle and the building of cycling paths as a solution to pollution. In Paris's case, this resulted in a local decrease in pollution, but an increase in pollution over the rest of the city. "Living well in the city", that has been a fundamental philosophical consideration since Aristotle does not refer to a tool or a material function, but a set of dynamic interactions that produces something as un-definable as "living well". This is a very real risk with digital technologies that, as we've seen, are somehow believed to be the way to build the perfect city.

A similar exercise was performed by the local government in Marseille on the theme of elderly people. A change in modern urban life is elderly people no longer with their children but rather live increasingly alone, away from their children. This phenomenon is now impacting Northern Africa where traditional family structures are changing, and also Asia (Singapore, for instance), where generational solidarity is traditionally very strong. The research showed that the quality of life of elderly people – as is the case for everyone, but particularly for old people – is linked to the quality and quantity of their social interactions. In the face of growing health problems, old people need "natural help" in the form of their loved ones who sometimes are far away. However, anyone can provide this natural help in response to difficult situations, and cities should be the perfect place to provide these interactions. Yet we can no longer count the number of cases of elderly people dying alone only to be found after several weeks when the smell alerts the neighbors.

The only possible interaction is then rescue services, when these people have difficulty getting around, whether due to physical or financial restrictions considering the low levels of retirements. This is a serious problem, and the number of calls to emergency services that then have to arrive on-site and help transport the person to a medical care center is growing. A trip to the hospital of this kind can cost around 300 euros in France, and contributes to saturating emergency services that must increasingly compensate for the lack of local care centers that can take care of minor issues.

The integration effort of functions, which will lead to the emergence "ageing well in the city", is represented in Figure 4.16. The function of production – the one that directly produces "growing old in good health" is the result of the integration of two functions, "life in the neighborhood", which allows interactions with natural help providers, and "health networks", which must be accessible. Are these two functions the product of integration of functions "housing" (does it favor help or urban solitude relations?), "work" ("work-sleep-repeat" does not favor neighborhood relations in dormitory cities), "transport" (are they accessible, do they reach appropriate areas?) and "health centers" (avoiding emergency rooms). The success of this integration rests on quality governing by whichever authorities define people's path through healthcare services, the latter which is defined by the territorial structure of the healthcare system that should offer at least three echelons of healthcare: clinics for minor problems, local hospitals for care and routine surgery, and large hospitals – for example *La Timone* in Marseille – for heavy surgery and vital pathologies. This

integration means accounting for residents' lifestyle and their healthcare needs. Integration will also be supplied by support functions: data collecting and processing (population healthcare, typical pathologies, behavioral analyses, etc.), and intervention processes (from rescue services,

SDIS = *Service départemental d'incendie et de secours* (Departmental Fire and Rescue Services) and SAMU = *Service d'aide médicale urgente* (Urgent Medical Aid Service), digital networks and programs).

This work helps define a system that is both efficient when it comes to generating comfortable ageing and in setting up coherent and effective rescue services that do not create extra expenses. We see that a function serves a number of ends and is made inoperable by digital technology and that the short-sightedness of accountants, who eliminated clinics in the name of pseudo-budgetary rationality, is not pertinent since they actually generate savings for hospital management and a greater efficiency for public services.

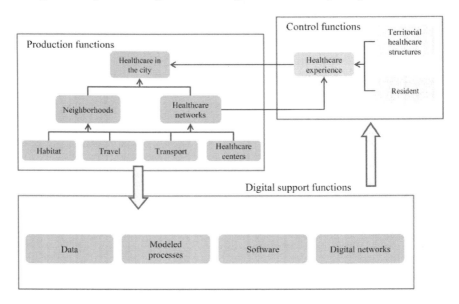

Figure 4.16. *Integrating a function "ageing well in the city"*

4.4.7. *Integrating heterogeneous systems*

This integration effort must remain conscientious of four particular points.

4.4.7.1. *Balancing the different dynamics of hard systems and soft systems*

Current prototypes of smart cities focus on hard systems, technological systems, and forget about the people, something we looked at earlier. Yet, people play a central role as they are the ones who will be using these technological systems and it is their behaviors that will decide whether the system is smart or not.

Figure 4.12 shows the integration of these two types of systems. We saw earlier that hard systems are not *conservative* in nature and can be described using the laws of physics, while soft systems are *dissipative* and cannot[21]. This is where we start to touch on the inevitably *political* aspect of smart cities: monetary and physical investments concern conservative systems, and the key to success lies in dissipative human systems formed by the users of these physical systems. If a city's design is left to industrial magnates, they will design it on the basis of hypotheses and behaviors that may ignore the turbulent and unstable reality of human systems. At worst, we are looking at a totalitarian regime or a utopic city containing only humans with flawless behaviors. Industry leaders must integrate this human component into their products, or they will inevitably be dysfunctional.

This is the whole problem of the current field of connected vehicles, which relies on a physical system that emits and receives assistance information to a driver, and, if the situation allows it, enables automatic piloting. However, what is possible for a plane traveling through a relatively stabilized and unchanging environment is far less for an automobile moving through an unstable and unpredictable environment, where any number of events can occur. If driving privilege has been granted to a technical system, this will lead to a decrease in driver vigilance when the latter is required to take control again. In practice, to this day, autonomous driving is only possible in a closed environment where unpredictability is limited.

---

21 A *conservative* system is close to a classic mechanical system. It is relatively closed and based on a fixed amount of energy that it will look to preserve. It tends towards the equilibrium. A *dissipative* system, conversely, is very open and exchanges a lot of energy (or information) with its environment. While the first is not very entropic, the second one is and will grow less and less balanced, meaning that it requires negentropy-creating governance to bring it back towards equilibrium.

Urban ecosystem

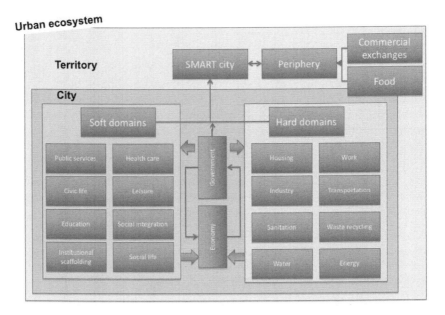

Figure 4.17. *A city is the integration of physical and human systems. For a color version of this figure, see www.iste.co.uk/rochet/cities.zip*

4.4.7.2. *Within/outside: defining system boundaries*

An urban system cannot be reduced to the city itself. It is integrated within a territory, which is in turn integrated within a regional system and, more broadly, a global system. Even in the case of a city-state such as Singapore, its leaders like to highlight that they are a smart *nation* and not just a smart *city*. A city exchanges with its periphery, which produces goods and services such as food, and with far-away territories following the principle of Thünen zones.

For an urban system to consider mastering its complexity, it is important that it defines what is within and what is outside of these various zones so as not to end up with a giant unstable system such as a megalopolis. We must therefore define the urban system that inherently has the most "eco" properties, an ecosystem capable of self-regulation and then the various circles of Thünen zones, and finally, exchanges with the rest of the world. Thünen zones define the relations between the urban ecosystem and activities tending towards less and less increasing returns, from an industrial or agricultural countryside to an extensive agriculture.

Exchanges represent the logistic and environmental costs. When the socialist mayor of Séné in Morbihan, right in the heart of Brittany where granite extraction is the main industry, prefers Chinese granite over Breton granite, which causes social and environmental costs in China where working conditions are far less favorable than in France, it destroys the granite industry in Brittany and generates social costs, in return for short-term savings. The more the perimeter is open, the less the system is stable.

4.4.7.3. *Combining top-down and bottom-up approaches*

Each industry now proposes its integration model. *Smart grids* (optimization of energy distribution networks), water management, transportation operators, digital network suppliers, etc., have their own model for integrating a sub-system into the urban system to evaluate its impact on the overall system. This is how we can assess the impact of installing a tram line on the overall transport flow in real time, and the model allows us to control the evolution of each operational and environmental parameter simultaneously.

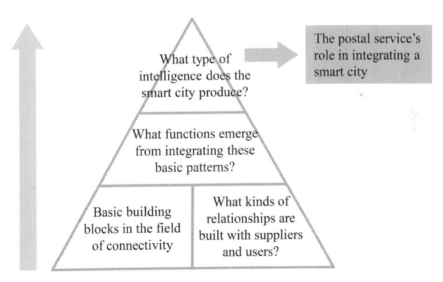

Figure 4.18. *Bottom-up integration of patterns*

However, we can go from the bottom-up in just the same way as playing with Lego, often starting to assemble them without really knowing what the end result will be. Smart city operators can gather and ask themselves "If we pool all of our offerings and integrate them together, what sort of city would that create?". Starting from a "triangular" integration structure (Figure 4.19) and following it upwards rather than downwards, according to the diagram in Figure 4.13, we will present the offer of each firm under the firm of patterns.

Such a project was organized by *La Poste* in the context of a strategy workshop around job reconfiguration and the future of its icon: the postal worker. There are fewer and fewer letters circulating with the rise in digital communication, but there are more and more packages due to the rise in e-commerce. For *La Poste*, its basic job must remain connecting people with one another, companies with one another, companies to people and vice-versa. In addition, in the countryside, the postman maintains a role in an essential social bond. *La Poste* wishes to think of its role as an operator for connection in tomorrow's smart cities.

A diverse panel of businesses was gathered in this workshop, transport, energy, construction, etc. Their offer was presented as a *pattern* around four questions: the context of the offer, the problem at hand, the description of the offer and the solution to said problem.

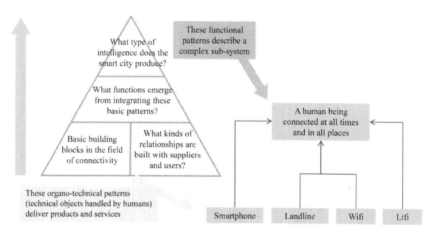

Figure 4.19. *An example of innovative emergence, integrating technical innovations in the field of digital transmission outlines a social "object": the individual connected at all times and in all places*

Next, through the course of a number of workshops, participating companies pool together their *patterns* and, as in a game of construction, by integrating them, built possible configurations that will constitute functions of the city (Figure 4.20). The point of this exercise is to promote the material production of businesses by linking it to functions likely to contribute to the quality of a city. In this way, we enter a virtuous cycle where the contribution to the common good conjugates with that of a business and in which all of them enter a coopetition mentality.

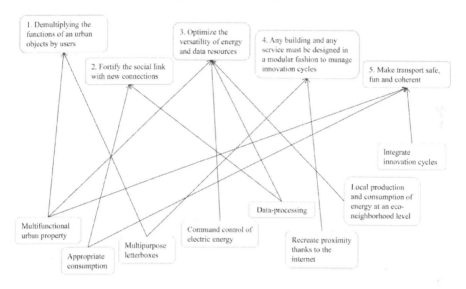

Figure 4.20. *Integration cycles: the patterns that represent the offer of participating offers by businesses are integrated to the propositions of city functions. Each pattern (at bottom) can be linked to a number of functional propositions (at top). An exercise in collective intelligence between participating businesses builds a common vision and operating model*

4.4.7.4. New business models

Firms will therefore be required to make global offers responding to the systemic character of city components. This is the principle of coopetition, or the combination of cooperation and competition. Businesses must define performance indicators that account for their own offerings' performance as part of a city's overall performance. Same goes for public management. In vertically arranged administrations, no one is in charge of the global vision of the city. In the setup of public markets, who will be in charge of purchasing a smart grid, or the running of a transport system? On the business side, the notion of extended business arises, that integrates one or more core companies and their partner networks that represent a value chain in the ecosystem. The same principle should apply to an administration. The break of the value chain perfectly demonstrates how the over-optimization of one part leads to the under-optimization of the overall system.

An attempt was made by businesses in the textile industry to establish new public purchasing procedures. The French administration clothes 1.5 million public servants, for example, with lab coats or sophisticated uniforms, right up to technologically advanced firefighting suits or mine-sweeper armors. The purchasing procedure currently takes the form of a bidding war that will only consider the cost and a few parameters around product quality and supplier reliability. This naturally leads to favoring offers that are based on low wages, with the effects that go with it such as lowered competitiveness of French firms. In this age of information technologies, textiles are also becoming "smart". Specialist clothing are laced with technologies and building a mine-sweeper armor or firefighting suit uses cutting-edge technology both for fabrics and other components involved in their fabrication. This industry employs approximately 800,000 people, most of them part of small and medium businesses, and if we look at other countries – the United States, for example – public power and businesses would cooperate through research contracts such as SBIR and would benefit from privileges stemming from SBA. However, in France, this is forbidden by European treaties. Each governmental purchasing act contributes to the country's own deindustrialization.

The public decision should therefore integrate all costs and indirect benefits, which we call externalities. Not only by taking into account all variables of the lifecycle of the product, which, in order to assess the cost of a digital device, is referred to as the *total cost of ownership* and includes maintenance, training, updates, energy use and cost of recycling. There is no such thing for smart cities. The French administration always reasons in terms of *sectors* (aerospace, automotive, etc.) and is very ill-equipped to understand the interdependencies between sectors. The extended administration is not a priority.

5

Smart City in Action

To this day, smart cities remain an ideal since none exist, except for Singapore perhaps, but there are many experiences that show that, on the one hand, the process has started, and on the other hand, the transition towards smart cities beyond its current market is a legitimate and obtainable objective. These experiences are the results of both intentional projects of constructing a smart city and unintentional creations since a smart city can grow organically. However, within the context of the third industrial revolution, radical innovations will be better valued in deliberate pilot projects.

5.1. Two cities that should not exist: Norilsk and Singapore

Two examples of cities that represent the divergence in cities founded on political impetus are Norilsk and Singapore. These two cities would have no reason to exist if nature had been left to its own devices. They are located in unlikely areas: Singapore is on the Equator, there is no drinking water, it has a humid, hot and unpleasant climate year-round and there was only one activity when it was founded in 1965, that is, the port left by the British. A typical example of a monotown! Today it is one of the most prosperous city-states in the world.

5.1.1. *Norilsk, the most polluted and polluting city in the world*

Stalin decided to build Norilsk in the 1930s, a city he wanted to be "as beautiful as Leningrad", in the Russian Arctic: 280 days of extreme cold,

130 days of snow-storms and 45 days of the polar night a year. Just like Saint Petersburg under Peter the Great, the city was built by slave labor since Norilsk was a gulag. It aimed to exploit mines of non-ferrous metals in the Great Siberian North. It only became a city in 1953, after the gulag was closed and 500,000 inmates had worked tirelessly in extreme conditions. Soviet authorities attempted to make it into a real city with model infrastructures and high salaries. Today, it is a closed city, with no communication other than by plane, with reserved access, mainly home to temporary workers and housing with just under 200,000 residents. It is the most polluted and polluting city in the world. While the workers are now there of their own free will and well-compensated, it still has a mono-activity.

Yet, its residents are quick to point out that it was close to becoming a real city:

> "Take an atlas of Siberia in 1914 and open the page on Taïmyr: you'll see that the peninsula was full of small black dots – villages. There were anywhere between 150 and 200 at the time. Whereas today, there are three cities in Taïmyr: Norilsk, Doudinka and Oust-Avam. There is a real difference in mentalities between the residents of Norilsk and Doudinka. In Doudinka, people are very attached to their city, but here people only stay for a short while. This is because Doudinka was built on the location of the old village of Doudinskiï, founded over 400 years ago. People have lived there for generations and are attached to the land. Norilsk, however, was founded in 1939 on virgin soil, 12 km away from Norilskiï, which gave it its name". [LEC 15]

In other words, there was, and there is, a social capital lying in the Russian Arctic, a people with its history and its traditions that are closely protected. Soviet power was able to make nothing where there was once something. In addition, residents taking part in the interview conclude *"Russia always needs to be directed manually"*. In sum, Norilsk did not develop endogenously.

(a)

(b)

Figure 5.1. *The two faces of Norilsk: October Square is part of an architectural success, an illustration of the construction on permafrost, but, the counterpart of a completely top-down design of the city is that many buildings are empty and run-down (photos credit: Elena Chernyshova)*

5.1.2. *Singapore, the smart nation*

The Singapore experiment is radically opposite. From the very start, Singapore was imagined by its founder, Lee Kwan Yew, as a *Smart city*, and furthermore as a *Smart nation*. What was a disadvantage became an advantage. Singapore has become something where in 1965 there was nothing more than a conglomeration of dirty houses. Singapore is today a city at the confluence of a multitude of activities, which very quickly embarked upon a digital revolution thanks to innovating policies. It is the result, on the one hand, of central planning or, better, global thinking, but, on the other hand, of one that constructs an institutional context that allows cities to develop around its residents' initiatives and lives. It is designed as a life system and not "machines for living in" in the style of Le Corbusier or Stalinist architects.

It is an example of functional integration that today allows complex systems modeling – that medieval art had intuitively understood. Housing, work and transport are designed in such a way that residents do not spend more than 45 minutes every day commuting, while residents of Mexico City will often spend up to four hours every day getting to and from work. Its famous artificial trees serve to collect rain water and solar energy, and provide climate control, CO_2 processing and pleasantness (Figure 5.2).

Figure 5.2. *Artificial trees in Singapore hold a number of functions: aesthetics, temperature regulation, collection of rain water, etc. (photo credits: Shiny Things)*

Two parallel paths, two diverging destinies: What is the take-away?

First, that a city's intelligence is its ability to grow organically and form a coherent ecosystem, economically and politically, and one that is able to evolve. What should we learn from the history of Singapore, which could be applied to Russia's archetypal obsolete urban fabric? Here are four main lessons:

Long-term planning relying on a strategic vision. As early as 1965, Singapore's visionary Prime Minister was imagining the growth of the city into a *smart nation*, meaning a global vision of the city as a generator of wealth and well-being – "A city in a garden" – driven by a high level of scientific knowledge helping to integrate technological advances. This vision translates to a 50-year plan, updated every five years to include new creations and unresolved problems and the possibilities offered by new technologies.

An efficient government plays an **integrative** role in urban functions. Singapore is an archetype of a development-oriented state, very interventionist, and a direct kind of interventionism so to speak from the foundation until the mid-2010s. It then gradually became more and more indirect as the economy grew, to define the institutional framework of the private sector's vitality. A very professional civil service works laterally around great urban functions. System architecture, as a method for project management is now fully mastered and allows digital technologies to be optimally used in projects centered around functional integration (for example, designing a commute to be under 45 minutes every day) and not technique itself, which allows a better articulation between public governance and deployment by public entities that boast failure rates far below the standards of industrialized countries. The BIM standard (*building information modeling*) is mandatory in construction to help integrate jobs from maintenance to design.

An articulation between the central role of the government and initiative of actors, a city is an archetype of the strategist state: the atmosphere is favorable to pilot and innovative field projects that are quickly integrated into the global system. To face an ageing population, Singapore implemented an alert system activated by the detection of any behavioral anomaly through multiple sensors that can be placed in households and public areas. Parents, but also any voluntary citizen, can sign up to become a natural care provider and intervene whenever an anomaly is detected. Technology, civism and traditional values are therefore integrated. Singapore is not a direct democracy, but a strong state where transgressions are immediately regulated (which, by definition, is the case for a self-regulating system such as a direct democracy), but considered legitimate by its citizens. As the country develops its social capital through education and investing in innovation, the government sees the need to encourage bottom-up dynamics resulting from social and civic initiative and release its grasp by developing multiple forms of decentralized participation.

Just like Norilsk, Singapore is not a natural city: considering its conditions, it should not exist. Its presence is the result of the political will to make it the smartest city in the world. This suggests *strategic state leadership and constant investment in innovation*. The success of the city stems from the legitimacy of its vision, which is very different from the case of Norilsk, because it is a shared vision in the case of Singapore. Conversely to what is suggested in predominant economic theory, Singapore's success is not due to the application of neo-liberal doctrines of free-trade and being open to the winds of globalization, but rather due to vision of the role of the state that is both systemic and pragmatic, described by Kishore Mahbubani, the director of the University of Singapore.

> "Asian governments have not looked at government as the problem. Instead, many were convinced that it can provide solutions. (...) Another damaging aspect of the Reagan–Thatcher revolution was the fundamentalist belief that "markets know best"(...). The obvious question in the minds of many Asians is: How could ideology have so blinded him to the realities of actual market functioning, which brought the world to the brink of a total meltdown? (...)
>
> In contrast to Greenspan's ideological views, most Asian policymakers traditionally worked on the pragmatic assumption that, in the real world, it was important to maintain a balance between the "invisible hand" of free markets and the "visible hand" of good governance.(...) . The "light-touch" regulation advocated by British and American regulators (in part, as a result of ideological assumptions of the Reagan–Thatcher revolution) has clearly failed. (...) Hence, one key struggle that Asian regulators are facing is how to find the right balance."

Finding the right balance in redesigning their financial architecture over the range of complex policy structures and issues mentioned above will be much more difficult for Asian policymakers in the postcrisis environment.

After this crisis, the importance of good, strong governance has come back with a vengeance. (...) In trying to find the right balance in redesigning the new financial architecture, the Asian governments know they must avoid both extremes: the debilitating heavy-touch nature of Soviet central planning as well as the irresponsible light touch of the Reagan–Thatcher revolution and financial market fundamentalism". [MAH 10]

From the very start, President Lee Kwan Yew understood the **dynamic of increasing returns** to finance the development of Singapore, shantytown in 1965. The vision was to build "a garden city" uniting both aesthetics and quality of life for its residents. The state is therefore both an entrepreneur as it invests directly and initiates projects, and an architect in that it sets meta-rules for developing the city, which are, in this case, very constraining in nature due to its limited geography, and also regarding the examples of catastrophic urban development in cities in Southeast Asia. The natural advantage offered by the port attracted foreign capital that was invested in local development. In doing this, the city-state increased its ability to attract big companies and so forth, the issue becoming how to maintain the city's coherence and the pace of its growth. Singapore dedicated the constitution of its education capital up to three times the amount of foreign direct investment. Accumulating innovations, the city is able to export them, improving its ability for self-financing. Development presents a new challenge at every stage, and while the city is now hailed as a visionary archetype of the globalized city, it does not escape the risks of social and spatial dysfunctionality present in globalized cities. This drift, dangerous if un-governed, is a governmental preoccupation in a culture centered around equilibria between opposing elements and that fears imbalance and disharmony. This is the new challenge for Singapore.

How can Russia learn from these lessons and turn the burden of monotowns into an opportunity for innovation? Russia is a laboratory for innovation with the renovation of "Kroutchevka" and "Brejnevka", these buildings similar to our great constructions of the 1960s, where the economic return of urban innovations can be very quick considering the energetic "abyss" that are these installations. An asset could be that the Russians think more in terms of "territory" than "city", which is the interdependence between a city and its outskirts, while we live in the illusion that a city can be green without ever considering that over 50% of its pollution is imported.

If Singapore is a reference as a smart city, it is that it was designed as such from the ground up. It is clear that it is far more difficult to do the same on constructed urban fabric. Christchurch in New Zealand is now joining the adventure, but only because... it was destroyed by an earthquake in 2011! Physically destroyed but maintaining the social capital of a population with strong traditions of civic involvement that is allowing a bottom-up redesign of the city.

Russian monotowns are a land of opportunity not only for investment and innovation, but also, and perhaps most importantly, for designing a way to transition from a dysfunctional urban fabric to a smart city, which is the question that is asked in emerging countries that will be the stage for urban growth over the next 30 years.

As with any complex project, it is important to start off with pilot projects such as R&D support that will help understand the dynamic of the urban fabric in a specific context. These projects will help stimulate the social capabilities that are at the core of the appropriation of an urban dynamic. The Russian federal government still dedicates US$520 million in social subsidies to monotowns that today no longer produce anything. Transforming these expenses into investments and adding foreign investments would make a return to increasing returns possible. Since the return of the State in Russia and the disappearance of the political power of the "seven bankers" (*Semibankirschina*) of the 1990s, a fabric of small and medium companies is growing. Russia does not yet have the culture of innovation and is low on the *Global Innovation Index*, but the scientific level there is excellent and we are seeing the appearance of the first technoparks. As for Singapore and China, foreign investment will be an opportunity to transfer technology and knowledge that will feed an endogenous growth, and help the development of "new city sciences".

The marginal cost of intelligence is in reality very low on an old urban fabric, since the expenses are generally fatal ones in infrastructure refurbishing expenses: performing these operations intelligently does not cost more than performing them unintelligently, but will reduce future costs a lot more! The marginal cost linked to new technologies does not generally exceed 10%, widely compensated by positive returns in the form of savings on energy, transport and the ability for innovation, which become a source of exportation, which is the case for Singapore, which after importing technology for a while, now exports it.

5.2. Pilot projects

A pilot project aims to test a hypothesis surrounding all or part of the systemic dynamic of a smart city. The ideal type of the pilot projects can resemble the establishment of a competitiveness cluster. There must be sponsors to support it and finance it. A *political sponsor* – a State, region, city, group of representatives, etc. – carries the political ends of the project, *the idea*, the vision that may still be slightly unclear but will become more and more defined as the project grows. The *industrial sponsor* is a collective of participating businesses that will test new technological solutions and the evolutions of their own business models and their industrial offerings. The third essential sponsor is *university research* to stimulate a scientific procedure independent of the industry to validate the scientific validity of the results. The role of the research is twofold in our case: on the one hand, it is the traditional role of research to create valid knowledge, but, on the other hand, the field we are dealing with is rife with all sorts of power groups looking for scientific justification and it is commonplace for them to offer funding to researchers in exchange for pre-validating their results. Karl Popper established in the 20th Century that science progresses by *falsifying* admitted truths, meaning that what we thought was true until now is no longer the case, not because it has always been "false", but because we have reached a superior level of truth. This supposes a confrontation process between research procedures and results of research with reality. A project's scientific council must be composed of true scientists recognized as such by the scientific community, publishing in scientific journals. Far too often, we see scientific councils composed of experts with varying degrees of expertise, but with no practical experience in research.

These three actors are linked by a consortium agreement that defines industrial and intellectual property laws and the way in which knowledge propagates. The pilot project in itself will have clearly defined objectives: if there are to be returns within an acceptable timeline and interpretable results, the project will bear on precise functions of the city and problems that can be clearly formulated. The device serves to nourish a virtuous cycle where market creation, knowledge creation and creation of competences are all working in synergy and reinforcing one another.

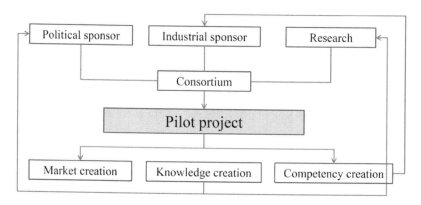

Figure 5.3. *Structure of a pilot project*

5.2.1. *The African city*

Africa is home to approximately 1.1 billion residents in 2017, of which 68% do not have access to water, and 80% of the rural population (600 million people) do not have access to electricity. The natural demographic growth in the continent due to high fertility levels with an average of six children per woman makes the African proportion of the world population in the decades to come alarming. The African urban environment is suffering from the consequences of this demographic growth, even though urban growth is mainly a result of migrations from the rural areas into the cities. Drought, environmental degradation, rural poverty and wars continue to force a great number of villagers to leave for the cities in order to search for other economic and social outlooks. Unfortunately, there is little work available, and this reality pushes city-dwellers to unusual initiatives of social self-innovation[1] pushed by a need for survival, curiosity or change.

---

1 A practice of individual response to one or more social requirements for a person or group of people.

This is how Nigeria, the Democratic Republic of Congo (DRC) and Ethiopia have begun to emerge as demographic powerhouses. According to the *Population Reference Bureau* (2015), in 2050, Nigeria will remain the number one African demographic power, ranked as the fourth most populated country in the world, with 400 million people. Congo will be in ninth position with approximately 90 million people, and Ethiopia will boast 165 million people.

Thus, the African continent, burdened by its demographic growth seems to march on like a sleepwalker towards a future of wasted opportunities and potential instability. Western countries are attempting to contain African migrations rather than to solve the underlying causes. This panorama reveals Africa as a continent that is suffocating under its own urgency. In addition, the time to act is running out. African cities are simply disoriented. They are overwhelmed by the speed at which these changes are occurring and have no control over them. Problems plaguing African cities do not simply stem from a lack of resources and services, but also stem from the severity of Africa's social disturbances, to high crime rates, levels of corruption and the inefficiency of local authorities. This all has repercussions on water services, electricity, schools and housing.

Smart city projects in Africa must therefore be global development projects that deal with the stability of the city as a sustainable ecosystem, creating economic opportunities, and the development of social capital. Africa has two options when it comes to smart cities: the one adopted by the Senegalese government that has launched a smart city project entitled *Diamniado Lake City* that has the ambition to rival the likes of New York, Beijing and Dubai[2]. "*Nothing will be too big or too beautiful*" states the Senegalese government that is granting the construction of the city to foreign investors for the sum of two billion dollars. A project that reeks of Richard Florida's "creative classes", except that this one intends to leave behind more than 70% of the population: the Senegalese people that work on the construction site have no access to water or electricity. This island of super rich amidst the poor will have its own business center, international airport, luxury apartments, renewable energies, etc., all while being financed by Chinese investors with no consideration towards the technological independence of the country.

---

2 For a presentation of the project, see [OUR 16].

The other option is that of endogenous development, which will integrate high-end technologies by absorption from the populations, from indigenous knowledge systems. To the Diamniado approach that begins from the top down without accounting for populations or territorial capital, are opposed bottom-up approaches that start from the reality of peoples' lives, in order to link it to high-end technologies through an endogenous and frugal process of innovation.

5.2.2. *The emergence of a territorial project through meaning: the case of Rhamna, in Morocco*

Moroccan researcher and consultant Amine Belemlih has implemented a novel approach, whereby he accompanied the emergence of a territorial collective project with sense-making dynamics, an example of a bottom-up design of a smart territory. In conjunction with the authorities of this small rural province on the Casablanca–Marrakech axis, Amine asked himself about the creation and development of economic and social fields, not in terms of a result of a national policy, but as the support for a regional project driven by its people, in other words, designing smart territorial specializations that would be driven by organic growth and catalyzed by territorial actors, NGO's local to agricultural cooperatives, private operators and local collectives.

The challenge is sizeable: **how does public decision, which necessarily comes from the top, meet organic dynamics that necessarily come from the bottom**? (Figure 5.4). This organic dynamic, when looked at closely, translates to individuals deciding to engage in a common action because it *makes sense* for them. At the same time, faced with the ambiguity of situations and diverging interpretations that people can make of them, there is no such thing as a plunge into reality through action, which is known as *enactment*[3], to assist this collective sense to emerge, refine and specify itself: this is one of the key concepts of social psychologist Karl Weick on

---

3 Readers rest assured; this has nothing to do with the French ENA! *Enactment* covers the processes of perception, selection and attribution of meaning to a reality. Inspired by Francisco J. Varela, American researcher Karl Weick [WEI 95] developed an original vision of social organizations where structures are placed in action at the same time as people are acting. He studies *sensemaking* or the ways in which people attribute meaning.

sensemaking, led over the past four decades [WEI 95]. *Enactment* consists of attempting to transform one's environment to understand it, which goes hand in hand with the famous quote by Kurt Lewin: *"If you truly want to understand something, try to change it"*.

The key question

→ How can a city that does not need a government be designed?

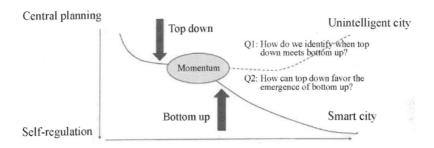

Figure 5.4. *The Gordian knot of smart city design: moving from central planning to self-regulation*

In the case of Rhamna, the question is to understand how a territorial network of actors around solidarity sectors can emerge. The objective is to identify the mechanisms, processes and *patterns* at work that allow such an emergence, with the aim to produce a model of this process that could be useful to other territorial emergences, by integrating contextual variables and specific objectives that can vary. We are in the perspective of a "metamodel" rather than a cooking recipe made of a protocol and purely predictive mechanisms. But what do we mean here by emergence?

> "Emergence is the creation of order, the formation of new properties and structures in complex systems. When emergence happens, something new and unexpected arises, with outcomes that cannot be predicted even from knowing everything about the parts of the system". [LIC 14]

This phenomenon, observed in physical and natural systems is also implemented at the organizational level, the level of collaborative communities and, moreover, the level of social systems. Numerous studies have been performed on these emergence phenomena, in particular the one on the city of Branson [CHI 04] as a major cluster of theater and music-hall performances, on regional clusters or industrial alliances such as the alliance in semi-conductors in the USA in the 1990s, to face the Asian markets [BRO 95]. These studies, to quote only a few, highlight a certain number of determinants and major characteristics of social emergences, in particular:

– the innovative character of the emergent system (not limited to the sum of the characteristics of individual components);

– the non-reducibility (to only the components of the system);

– the reciprocal causality (emergent properties have a bottom-up, top-down and lateral influence on the components of the system and the latter have an influence on the overall system);

– the increased capacity of the system resulting from this emergence dynamic (the same goes for the amplifying effect of the immaterial capital that develops within a cluster of innovation, for example).

What specifically interests us here is that at the core of social emergence is a continuous current of interactions linking a large number of individuals. Each interaction is activated by organizational forms already in place. The result is a current of involuntary or unintentional emergent structures that appear to restrict behaviors while giving meaning to human action. The same goes for local initiatives around *solidary actions*, which end up being reinforced by other spontaneous actions to the point of influencing the installation of secondary care centers, etc., giving an aspect of destination or specialization to a particular neighborhood.

A solidary sector is composed of activities that generate revenue developed in the dynamic of a virtuous ecosystem in the context of specific economic sectors, responding to the criteria of the *Economie Sociale et Solidaire* (solidarity and social economy), in particular the importance of the social bond, of cooperation, transparency, equality between people involved in exchanges, all along the economic value chain. This echoes a similar concept of "short solidary economic circuits" that favor social bonds, cooperation, transparency and equality between people involved in exchanges.

There can be an *intentionality of actions* at the beginning, impacting local institutional leaders or simple citizens and the entrepreneurial energy invested in this action, which imbalances the established order of things, stimulating their evolution. These actions end up being self-sustaining, driving the social system, at the scale of a neighborhood or a territory, in a new stable state, even though it is always "far from the equilibrium".

These dynamics of social and organizational emergence go through various phases.

First of all, the social ecosystem evolves towards a state of imbalance: in the case of Rhamna in Morocco, an alarming observation made by the community was that *"we cannot go on this way"* and that the endemic poverty of local populations, combined with failed local initiatives to develop alternative cultures, called for new ways of doing things that would break the mold. Then comes a phase of launching experimental energy-based actions that literally come and put stress on the system and engage fluctuations in an established order until reaching a threshold: this is the activism of NGOs, cooperatives and local economic operators instigating RGA (Revenue Generating Activities) and incubating new solidary sectors, with a heavy institutional support from the Governor. It is in this context that begins a "Rhamna hive", a social, provincial, entrepreneurial incubation space, and also the launch of pilot projects of solidarity sectors in chicken and alpine goat farming (yes, indeed, in Morocco) with a strong social dynamic of sensitization of women led by local associations.

The next phase, still currently emerging at the time of writing (2018), is that of *nonlinearity*, where the positive feedback loops amplify fluctuations, leading to the progressive advent of a new order. For example, in this case, this amplification has taken the form of growing interest from institutions such as the *Agence Française de Développement*, the World Bank, the Moroccan Ministry of Agriculture and the heads of various neighboring communities to take part in this provincial transformation project, articulated around pilot projects and an integrative and systemic procedure that is implemented as time goes on. One amplification leading to another, Moroccan business owners (CGEM), through their *Observatoire des*

Branches Professionnelles et des Régions (Observatory of Professional Branches and Regions), even offered to make this province a pilot territory in matters of *smart territorial specializations*, moving towards the emergence of an actual pole of excellence in social and solidary economy.

The third phase is recombining the existing elements (resources, expertise, partners, tools or methods, for example) as a means of increasing, through the acts of synergy and positive side effects, the potentialities of the social collective in emergence. This harkens to the works on *autopoiesis* by Varela [VAR 79]. In this case, the different action programs unite with others' projects: bridges appear continuously between initiatives to give birth to *meso-initiatives* that are constantly being improved and generating increasing momentum from local operators and institutional partners. In Rhamna, this gave birth to pilot projects of new solidary sectors or even new Moroccan regions, such as the region of Smara in the South of Morocco or Marrakech, interested in engaging in similar initiatives with their own stakeholders.

The fourth and final phase of this process is an emergent equilibrium that crystallizes certain institutional or organizational routines. This guarantees that the flow of resources injected into the system is uninterrupted: Rhamna's history is still being written.

The intention of the ongoing research project is to detect how collective mechanisms of meaning occur during the different phases of emergence, in order to identify the potential patterns allowing us to understand how involved parties make sense of their actions and how these actions lead to experimenting, organizing adapting, etc., the emergent social system in a recursive fashion. This experimental approach aims to enrich existing leadership models by placing them in a tradition of collective construction [LIC 09].

The contribution of the efforts by Amine Belemlih, a research-action project led with the support of the *Université Paris-Dauphine*, aims to produce a model for the process of emergent meaning in action within the emergence of a social territory. A contribution that is still unfolding, capital for any smart city developer.

5.2.3. *Casablanca as a prototype for remedying to the tentacular growth of cities*

Casablanca extends over 300 hectares per year. This is the manifestation of the law expressed by West and Bettencourt[4], the oil-slick extension of a city if nothing is done to prevent it. It is a polluted city, and we can only approximate its number of residents due to the considerable rural exodus and the amount of informal housing. The urbanization model in Morocco generally occurs by "playing catchup": take into account the inflation in population, proliferation of informal housing, shantytowns that are constantly being urbanized. The process is endless.

Driven by Electrical Engineering Professor Aawatif Hayar, at the University of Hassan II, who directs the research center *GreenTIC*, the Casablanca smart city project was made a reference project for Africa by the IEEE institute to design a reference model for Africa in order to remedy the situation. Supported by State authorities in the region and the city, the Casablanca smart city project piloted by Aawatif Hayar adopts an approach based on organic growth.

Her premise is the following considerations. In emerging countries, the concept of smart cities is even more pertinent than in developed countries under the double constraint of a high demographic growth and limited resources. The low cost or frugal approach to smart cities that she is offering involves using Information and Communication Technologies (ICT) to effectively use the limited resources of the city and the country. The idea is to represent another alternative for these cities in emerging countries in order to benefit from solutions offered by the concept of the smart city and its inherent dynamic for wealth creation and resource optimization without having to wait to have a large budget available. The basic idea is to create a virtuous cycle starting with people's needs and optimizing available means to better respond to expectations, opening new perspectives and creating wealth that generates more wealth via proximity.

This new model of the smart city is essentially centered around its people as primary operators of a sustainable and equitable development. It uses

---

4 See section 2.1.

digital tools combining the advantages of being both mobile and ubiquitous, which Aawatif Hayar sums up using the neologism *mobiquitous*, to offer services that are useful to citizens and collect data that is then processed and analyzed to offer other more appropriate services in the aim of a sustainable and equitable global social prosperity.

Emerging nations are faced with the same challenges as developed countries, insecurity, pollution, criminality, transport, housing, education, health, access to water and generally to what Amartya Sen calls *capacities*, that is, the real capacity to implement multiple "rights of" and "rights to" promoted by international organizations, but in a far more intense manner and with fewer resources, notably digital ones, with African countries being far less connected.

Morocco was able to get into the digital race in time. It is a country where the central power – the King – is very enterprising, in a top-own philosophy, which presents problems with relations with the territory in a country that has almost no middle class and where inequality is high, in particular in terms of education between the ruling class and the people. Thus, in 2013, the king launched the Casablanca smart city project.

The workgroup led by Prof. Hayar used a bottom-up approach to balance the State's top-down one. Inspired by experiments in developed countries and keeping in mind the limited means and infrastructures of emerging countries, she proposed to limit investment costs by using existing infrastructures, in particular *mobiquitous* ones such as smartphones and other mobile terminals for developing apps, services and pilot sites and thus creating the building blocks of a smart city, which would then be reinforced by other realizations until creating an interconnected environment. The need for connectivity guaranteeing the development of a positive digital experience is indispensable to help keep the citizens of the future involved and allow them to appropriate the data and services available to develop other innovations and other added value services.

This model, named *Ville Intelligente Sociale et Frugale* (smart, social and frugal city), has the following characteristics:

– adopting a participative and equitable e-governance continuously assessed according to performance indicators defined by a global strategy and vision of a smart city;

– encouraging social innovation to better respond to the needs of citizens;

– encouraging all actors of society (citizens, researchers, small to medium businesses, start-ups, etc.) to develop services and pilot experiences for smart cities;

– improve the well-being of residents and their involvement in the development of their city;

– minimizing costs of deployment and maintenance of a smart city by adopting economic mechanisms and models that favor its sustainability;

– developing sustainable approaches for extracting;

– encouraging innovation through the model of "open data for economic development" [OEC 15];

– transforming the city into a living experimental laboratory on the principle of the living labs that help develop local abilities and enrich R&D and innovation with terrain-based experience and data;

– adopting an evolving digital transformation of society and economics;

– using *mobiquitous* objects and networks (omnipresent and mobile) to develop services to residents based on digital technology;

– adopting incentivizing economic models based on crowdsourcing and crowdfunding.

These initiatives are integrated into a living labs[5]-type platform. It currently drives a number of projects surrounding Casablanca, in the housing sector, creating revenue-generating activities, in particular the objective of sustaining this project culture with the appropriation of certain technologies around development objectives.

---

5 *"A Living Lab is an open innovation research method that aims to develop new products and services. The approach promotes a process of co-creation with its end-users, under real-life conditions and also relies on an ecosystem formed of public-private-citizen partnerships. The Living Lab phenomenon was initiated in the late 1990s at the MIT Media Lab, and then developed further in Europe with the creation of the 2006 European Network of Living Labs (ENOLL) and there are now more than 340 Living Labs in more than 40 countries worldwide"* in [DUB 14].

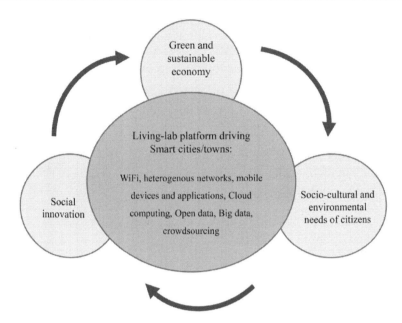

Figure 5.5. *Living labs platform of pilot projects for the Casablanca smart, social and frugal city project (source: Professor Aawatif Hayar, University Hassan II)*

This first family of projects aims to create a living social fabric in the city, beyond the magma created by the appearance of shanty towns due to informal housing. This is to help the city, in the long run, to develop a self-regulating characteristic, to understand its dynamic in order to define evolution diagrams that block oil-slick development and remedy the plagues of cities.

However, the other aspect of the Casablanca smart city program is remedying the exodus from the country to the city. One problem that can occur with the development of smart cities is the risk of excluding city outskirts from development, which will only reinforce rural exoduses. To do this, the *e-douar* project was launched. It consists of developing a transition zone between a smart city and its environment, to promote human development and create revenue-generating activity, because residents do not leave the countryside because cities are attractive, but because rural life is unattractive. By combining digital technology, alternative energies and ecological construction, the hypothesis is to develop revenue-generating activities, employment, and, at the same time, increase the attractiveness of these areas by developing tourism. The development of basic infrastructures and basic digital services could not only encourage the sustainability of rural housing, but also attract "rurban" residents and organize a "soft transition" between city and country.

The e-douar project is a research-action project that brings together residents in the *douar* and the University Hassan II. Digital technology is a resource for development and not a *deus ex machina*, which will inherently provide well-being by itself. The project will test the impact of implanting digital in a rural territory, through an approach based on the appropriation of these technologies by the people to create the uses that they deem pertinent for their development. The idea is therefore to organize a fusion between the realm of digital and indigenous knowledge systems. Here, digital is a base – represented by the smart house that concentrates all activities made possible thanks to digital technology – that allows the development of projects such as a biogas project that uses methane production from organic waste to produce energy for domestic and agricultural activities, while producing quality fertilizer. Digital technology will also help map agricultural lands to develop precision farming, thus reducing the use of fertilizer, optimizing water and cultures.

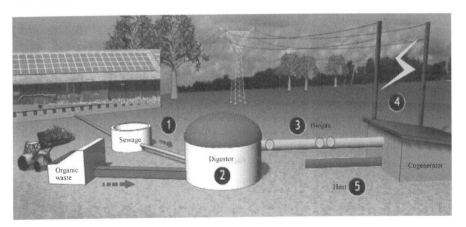

Figure 5.6. *One of the eDouar projects, local production energy from organic waste (source: Professor Aawatif Hayar, University Hassan II). For a color version of this figure, see www.iste.co.uk/rochet/cities.zip*

5.2.4. *Angola, Namibia: eco-design of a drinking water supply*

Dr Morris Zombo Mussema is an agricultural engineer and Angolan academic. He is heavily involved in the development of municipal communities in response to the shortage in water, a subject that was at the center of his thesis [ZOM 17a]. His action-research consisted of developing a water supply based on indigenous knowledge (similarly to the *"révolutions tranquilles"* (calm revolutions) described by Bénédicte Manier), and also basing it on a reproducible scientific model.

Beyond Information and Communication Technologies, a sustainable development approach to certain projects can convert a city into a smart city, integrating aspects of governance, demographic and economic dynamics in a way that is appropriate to the concerned social capital. This case study of an Angolan municipality touches on the deployment of the use of indigenous knowledge and key tools in the drinking water sector, and discusses best practices for resource management, in particular towards water offered by nature to satisfy human needs.

5.2.4.1. *A smart city in Africa: mirage or opportunity?*

In the decades to come, the populations of developing countries will also aspire to live in cities that are said to be smart. The latter are characterized by their modernism and sustainability, but also by the interconnectivity of the services they offer. Modernizing a city goes through technological innovation. As soon we acknowledge that within the word *"techno-logy"* is the word *logos*, knowledge, over the word *techné,* this innovation can be integrated advantageously into a territory. On the flipside, it can act against it when the technological choice is not appropriate or able to take root on the natural or social capital of the territory being modernized.

In a number of sectors, like that of drinking water, African municipalities, in particular in Angola and the DRC, even though they are equipped with a number of technologies have been surprised more than once and had to inherit the negative consequences caused by their hierarchical decision makers, suppliers, or service-providers supposedly experts who failed to account for the social capital and the characteristics of African urban sociology.

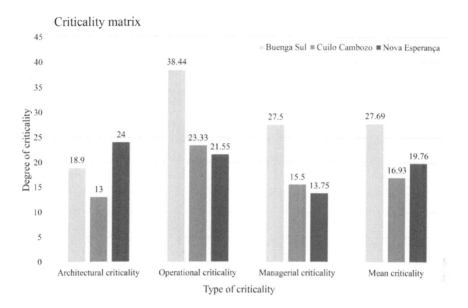

Criticality matrix

Figure 5.7. *A visual histogram of the criticality matrix of existing water systems*

Drawn in by a mirage that has failed to lead them to a sustainable smart city that they have been dreaming of, these municipalities were made into the recipients of public services that were losing their resilience and efficiency beyond the limits of criticality. Having pointlessly consented to colossal investments in high-risk technologies, they were then called in by their superiors to ask why the water system did not work properly. It is only after measuring the criticality of their failing water systems that the municipalities that were approached during this study realized that the answers to these questions could only be found by deploying a reliability metric each time they committed to installing a new water system.

In the Angolan case, the decision makers such as the users of the water services joined this study and agreed to assess the criticality[6] of their systems in the hopes of producing an analysis of the situation that may enlighten

_____

6 The criticality approach comes from the FMECA (Failure mode, effects, and criticality analysis) and finds its roots in the US military in the 1940s. It is a method that allows us to identify possible failures in military operations. We have adapted it to apply it to water sector, in order to assess the operation of a water system.

them. After this, to quantify this criticality, the severity of various failings identified in said systems were multiplied by their occurrence and their detection, while accounting for a set of 36 parameters, spanning the five primary operations of a water supply system. The criticality of any dysfunctions in the water systems is represented in the histogram in Figure 5.7: the very high criticality numbered at 27.69 for the locality of Buenga Sul, 16.93 for Cambozo and 19.76 for Nova Esperança on a scale where the acceptable range is between 1 and 11, showing us that these systems have only maintained an identity-based resilience. By "identity-based resilience", we mean a critical usage model beyond the normal capacity for resilience of a system.

They were unable to absorb any sort of disturbance, reorganize and continue to operate in accordance with the principle of sustainability and expectations of its users (which is an average delivery of 6 liters of water per day, per person). These results show us that just for the function "water", a function that is highly critical in Africa considering that only 42% of the population has access to it, we are currently far from smart cities being a viable opportunity.

5.2.4.2. A dynamic of territorial intelligence

The role of the dynamic of territorial intelligence is to integrate sustainable technologies into the territory and not the other way around. Recent experiments in certain African countries such as Buengas in Angola and Mosango in the DRC are prime examples of this. Hence, the Angolan municipality of Buengas solved its water supply problem by relying on an *endogenous production system of indigenous knowledge*. Its native communities have managed to make drinking water both a commodity and a factor of economic development rooted in the social capital of the territory. Such an approach has led the municipality to realize that, while financing from the State for the implementation of water supply services can play an essential role, the active participation of local communities is just as important, if not more. Given the extreme poverty in African cities, any sustainable solution to the problems faced by lower-income populations will use an integrated approach relying on community participation.

The resolution of a number of problems these cities are encountering depends heavily on not only these capabilities, the ability and legitimacy of institutions and municipal authorities, but also the quality and sustainability of selected technologies to attempt to promote them to the rank of the smart cities of tomorrow. This durability depends on the quality of the interface between technologies and social capital (culture, formal and informal institutions, level of education, etc.). Thus, the importance of integrating as many urban stakeholders as possible into modernization programs of the city; local authorities must be efficient, open and transparent. However, cities do not possess the administrative capabilities that would allow them to make good decisions on the lifestyles of their populations and therefore are exposing themselves to the risk of having to face popular demands. Seeing as more and more African people are moving to the cities, it is highly probable that these disowned populations will start requesting improvements to the situations of their cities. African local authorities are increasingly having to deal with requests from urban populations, catalogued in a reference sheet of stakeholders that must by all means be included in design models to solve the problems of cities.

5.2.4.3. *Towards a frugal "smart city"*

The Angolan failures recorded in the three villages of Buengas allow us to propose a design model[7] of eco-efficient water-supply systems for rural towns in developing countries. This model has generated three tools, two of which are managerial in nature and one that is technical. Among them there is (i) the criticality metric we mentioned earlier, (ii) the reliability index (*ZOMBO Index*[8]) as well as (iii) the blue pump, which is the frugal innovation derived from this research.

---

7 See Figure 5.8.

8 ZOMBO Index: (*Zéro Omission Managériale pour la Bonne Optimisation*), translates to Zero Managerial Omission for Proper Optimization, or shortened to **"Iz"** and is "the ecological ratio attributed to a drinking water supply proportionally to the material, financial and human resources invested in its implementation and the social, economic and environmental effects produced by this system".

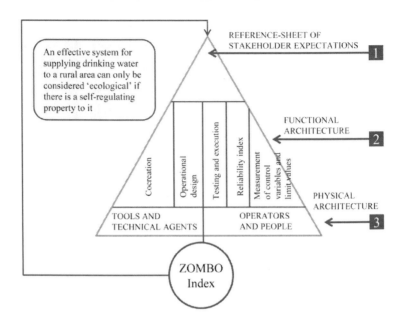

Figure 5.8. *Design model of eco-efficient systems for supplying drinking water*

The model is characterized by the fact that it references the expectations of stakeholders based on the indigenous system of knowledge production, the functional architecture of said model, the physical architecture of a typical water system to implement. The critical elements taken into account during the creation of this model are those coming from the indigenous knowledge production approach under the *Arbre à Palabres*[9] as well as the production, processing and distribution operations of water. The design approach we used for this model establishes specific objectives, creates a checklist of all possibilities and subsequently determines the requisite improvements for the definition and characterization of scalable models applicable to developing countries.

---

9 The *Arbre à palabres (palaver tree)* is the traditional location in an African village where the villagers would gather in the shade of a giant tree to discuss the issues within a community. It was a lever for social mobilization towards economic development as it allowed villagers to have open debates about subjects that were preoccupying them, about their needs and to find solutions to problems that were holding the village back. Furthermore, it helped them to imagine paths for economic development in all sectors.

The index that results from the formula presented below (see Figure 5.9) is driven by an eco-design approach fed by 96 parameters considered as critical to a water supply chain due to be eco-efficient, able to prequalify any new water system prior to its implementation, as either very risky, risky or even conversely as a veto. What we call VETO is actually the limits imposed on our model by the complexity of its environment.

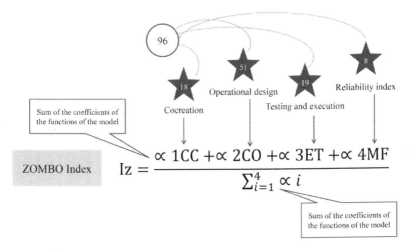

Figure 5.9. *Formula for calculating the eco-efficiency index of a drinking water supply system*

Of course, this formula used by researchers and engineers was translated into common vernacular allowing users to use simple questions relying on directly observable elements to assess the quality of the eco-design approach and the reliability of the system in place.

In Quipedro, a new location fitted with a novel water system eco-designed within a participative approach and thanks to a frugal innovation known as *the blue pump*, the level of performance reached by the water system is excellent. It is very reliable and operational 24/7. Fitted with environmental technology, easy to install and acquire, causing no pollution, boasting low maintenance costs and an approximate useable life of 50 years, without outflow of currency, this pump uses only indigenous resources. It would be one of the most precious gifts one could offer future generations of developing countries, in particular in rural cities, all of this within the limits of criticality.

Figure 5.10. *The blue pump (photo credits: Dr Morris Zombo Mussema)*

In Angola, the study demonstrated that it is possible to optimize the performance of water services thanks to new technologies on condition they be sustainable and the use of water responsible. However, despite consented investments, the urgent need to update the access to water purification installations and intensify hygiene practices in order to extract as many advantages as possible from these services, remains. Here and for other villages in the Southern Hemisphere, the water sector remains critical, and requires sustainable technologies that will ensure large-scale distribution. In search of solutions adapted to local contexts, the authorities can call upon the principles of smart cities... on condition that they obey the principle of frugality[10].

Nowadays (2018), Namibia is offering Dr Zombo Mussema a position as Professor at a top French University, to replicate the blue pump in the arid context of the country. The hydraulic motor of the blue pump will have to be replaced with a solar motor, possibly coupled with wind-farm technology, which is the local free energy in Namibia for extracting water from

10 See [ZOM 17a, ZOM 17b].

underground. As the pump is designed with modularity in mind, all that is needed is to invent a solar motor using the same principles: the blue pump will become the yellow pump, but the principles of eco-design will be the same.

5.2.5. *Urban problem and economic transition: the Russian case of monotowns*

Detroit in the USA, Turin in Italy, and Sochaux, Thionville, Florange and Le Creusot in France are – or have been – monotowns. These mono-industrial cities, with activities relying on a single industry and with residents that had only a single skill, are inherent to the capitalism of the second industrial revolution (1870–1971). The phenomenon is inherent to the silo-structured mass production model, where large companies are the common method of research for productivity increases. This production model has since become obsolete with the transition to the third industrial revolution that relies on technologies with a higher technological intensity, diversified with network relays of generally medium-sized businesses (even though sometimes they can remain organized around a single core company with a smaller size), and where innovation and diffusion of knowledge play a critical role.

In Russia, monotowns are born of both the capitalist tendencies of the authoritarian State that once was the USSR, the specificity of Russia's social history and its historical and geographical contingences. They are created near prime resources in Siberia, in the Ural, in the Arctic, in an economy mostly based on primary activities. Some of them started out as gulags, such as Norilsk (located north of the arctic circle). They also resulted from the outsourcing of industries threatened by the German advance in 1941 when they were actually moved east (which at the time was a remarkable feat).

5.2.5.1. *Monotowns: a phenomenon exacerbated by Russia's history*

Russian urban culture diverges from Western culture and has never been a lever for modernization. Russian cities have specific characteristics that find their source in the country's economic and social history. Thus, Russia never got urban civilization the way Europe did: urban development came late, towards the second half of the 19th Century. Urban growth and the appearance of a middle class and an urban civilization carrying its own civic culture never assimilated the way it did in Western Europe. Russia's autocratic system never saw an urban civilization that would drive communal liberty and autonomous urban life relating to commercial, industrial and political development when, paradoxically, Russia during the middle ages presented one of the most accomplished and early forms of direct democracy and urban liberty: the *Veche*[11]. These popular gatherings were born in the towns of Pskov and Veliki Novgorod[12] (located in the northeastern part of modern-day Russia), which were subsequently crushed by Tsar Ivan III in 1478.

After that, Russian cities were virtually indistinguishable from the country, as it did not move away from Feudal power. The effects on the urban development of industrial growth at the end of 19th Century were destroyed by civil war and the physical disappearance of what little historical working class was left, with the demographic crash of cities in the 1920s. The intense development during the Soviet era of industrialization was, according to the expression of Sociologist and Demographist Anatoli Vichnievski [VIC 00], but the "suburbanization" of the city, populated by farmers and where Soviet leaders knew they could not afford the appearance of urban emancipation. Thus, for Vichnievski, the Russian Revolution and its industrialization were a "conservative modernization". Following this reasoning, Soviet urbanization was but an instrument, a by-product of industrialization that needed "machines for living", rather than a lever for economic and political development. It remained conservative in fear of the emancipative effect of the city – "*Stadt Luft mach frei*[13]".

In the 1950s and 1960s, it pursued this top-down policy according to Le Corbusier's principles of functionalism. The latter collaborated, among other ventures, with architect Boris Rubanenko, master of Soviet architectural thought, to design the city of Togliatti using American principles of *urban planning*. For the Marxist philosophy that was incarnated in Rubanenko, the creation of a new city should occur in rupture with the *bourgeois* heritage of the past. This illustrated a convergence in Western and

---

11 The *Veche* (вече) was a very pure form of direct democracy that can be found today in the *landsgmeinde* of Swiss-German districts, where whoever rang the bell could call an assembly to deliberate on a subject. A common notion of common good and a global aesthetic tied to democratic deliberation helped resolve problems with the organization of urban functions (job organization, traffic, interfaces between towns and cities, religious and civic life) or even to choose and oust a Prince.

12 "Novgorod the Great", not to be confused with Nijni Novgorod.

13 "City air makes you free", German proverb from the middle ages.

Eastern urban philosophy, the West bringing its technicity and the East offering its political vision of urbanism meeting in a form of functionalism. Togliatti was supposed to be a city regrouping all industrial, housing and leisure functions, which could be covered on foot, incarnation of Soviet urban lifestyle. Khrushchev-era and subsequently Brejnev-era constructions were a progress in that they gave access to household comfort and moved away from community housing. However, these "machines for living" do not constitute systems of life. As Anatoli Vichnievski explains *"it seems that, by all standards, the Soviet society of the 1980s has become an urban society, but the reality is much more complicated than that"*.

The notion of urban systems being autonomous systems of life and development was therefore absent from Russian history before and during the Soviet period.

5.2.5.2. *Monotowns, a high cost and a threat*

Officially, the current number of monotowns in Russia is between 332 and 400. They are home to 15% of Russia's population and make up 30% of Russia's GDP [KIR 14]. They are not all in crisis: Norilsk remains one of the world's greatest producers of nickel, which represents 2% of Russia's GDP… However, it is also the world's most polluted and polluting city! In Togliatti (Russia's Detroit), Renault took over the Avtavaz factory, in hopes to resurrect it.

These towns are corporate cities, with a weak municipal administration, with no great ability or autonomy. Furthermore, these "dormitory-cities" age badly and are very costly to maintain. If the economic activity is failing – the 2008 recession hit Russia hard – businesses are no longer investing in infrastructure, salaries fall (they fell by a total of 14% following the 2008 recession), housing quality degrades and cities enter a vicious cycle of degradation. This is why Russian monotowns today are ticking time bombs of social and political troubles, especially considering the federal government unlocked over five billion dollars to sustain them, while choosing to let most of them wither and die. However, beyond this conjunctural dimension of managing the social crisis, we see Russia's economic reconversion towards the third industrial revolution.

5.2.5.3. *The Russian government's active policy*

We cannot consider maintaining these monotowns using subsidies, as was once the case – and still is. In France, this was once the case in Lorraine. The role of public financing was positive in that it maintained an effective industrial tool. However, in the long term, it delayed the reconversion of steel-work and had a considerable social and economic cost through a public device, the CGPS (*convention générale de protection sociale*), signed for this sector. Nonetheless, we can still consider it a success: the transformation of the business model for steel-work and the evolution of these production processes have made it a competitive company, accompanied with an urban renaissance. No industry, no territory is therefore condemned if it is able to reinvent itself using its past accomplishments.

In 2014, The Russian government created the monotown reindustrialization fund[14], a non-profit organization tasked with helping these towns to develop a new industrial model. Its policies rely on two main principles:

1) Finance only new projects that are not related to the core business of the monotown, with participation from the city of at least 5%, a principle-based partnership considering the financial weakness of monotowns. If the fund participates in a new company, the latter must remain a minority shareholder, at a maximum of 49%. The projects concern the requisite infrastructures for welcoming new businesses. Sixty-two regions had entered agreements in this way with the fund by the end of 2016.

2) This supply of industrial capital is reinforced by a development of human capital by the formation of project teams composed of representatives of regions and businesses: 227 teams will have completed a 250 hour course in Skolkovo by the end of 2017.

The advantage of this approach is that it moves away from subsidies aimed solely at survival to create conditions for the development of new activities in the cities in question as well as encouraging assistance and governance from the center – which was the norm in Russia since far before the Soviet era, almost as far back as Peter the Great.

---

14 Фонд развития моногородов (Fund for the Development of Single-industry Towns), http://www.frmrus.ru.

Industrial diversification is sought after when developing technoparks, which are supposedly a replication of *clusters* policies, uniting small and medium businesses, large companies, universities and investment banks into a common ecosystem. Such an approach is likely to stimulate a dynamic of territorial development. It is associated with certain mistakes that, despite recent progress, have not been resolved: weight of structures that are often mere window-shops designed to encourage investment and subsidies even though they offer no scientific or industrial added-value[15], an intransigent and air-tight bureaucracy inherited from the Soviet era, an absence of a specialized banking system and the persistence of a level of corruption, an under-developed judicial system for the protection of property laws. Furthermore, the institutional context is even more incomplete despite spectacular successes such as the technopark in Novossibirsk.

The approach that consists of considering urban development and industrialization as a form of endogenous dynamic rather than the result of an exogenous central initiative is still in gestation in Russia. The creation of what should have ended up being the Russian Silicon Valley in Skolkovo has turned out to be very disappointing. The project was handed to one oligarch, Viktor Vekselberg, who is ill-versed in the dynamic of innovative systems. There was an attempt to "copy and paste" infrastructures without understanding that the key to success is in the endogenous dynamic of an innovative ecosystem. It is not just a matter of placing people together in the same spot for creative interactions to occur. It requires a favorable context, something that research has described as a *"milieu innovateur"* (innovative environment), composed of conditions both material and immaterial. Having the right ingredients is a necessary condition for making a good mayonnaise, but actually making it remains subject to a sequence of events and conditions that can be hard to reproduce, just like a chef's technique. If we forget this, we are bound to re-enter a classic scenario of inefficient megastructures on a bedrock of corrupt business.

The conditions for progress are nonetheless present: international sanctions and drops in oil prices create a very favorable situation by cutting Russia off from the possibility of an economy based on exporting raw materials and importing foreign technologies, and by inciting the development of a national industry based on innovation.

---

15 Phenomenon known in France with the policy of competitiveness clusters.

Therefore, the matter of monotowns today offers us a concentrate of a Russia that is archaic and one that is ready to innovate and determined to rise to the challenges before it, but History tells us that the ability of the Russian man to rise to a challenge has rarely proved wrong/been caught.

5.2.5.4. *Smart cities: lessons learned from monotowns*

The transition from monotowns to smart cities concentrates all of the challenges of an innovative policy for entering Russia into the circle of big players in the third industrial revolution.

The Russian Federation was ranked 48th among the top 50 high-revenue nations by the 2015 Global Innovation Index, with the following strengths: education and scientific level, technological production; and weaknesses: the institutional and regulatory context, an insufficient transmission of scientific knowledge from universities to businesses; and very weak points: access to lending. The result of this environment is an insufficient dynamic of small to medium businesses that are at the core of innovation and that find its very source in the absence of an entrepreneurial dynamic in Soviet Russia. With the institutional collapse of Russia during the post-Soviet era, this entrepreneurial dynamic that is at the heart of innovation was only able to start again during the 2000s, and was still impeded by a badly adapted institutional framework.

Using the transition from monotowns to smart cities as a structuring axis for monotowns helps integrate all of these aspects into an urban policy based on organic city development, to go from a governance model exclusively from the center to a system that favors endogenous development of the territory.

This problem occurs similarly in France, through the example of the reconversion that took place in the Choletais, around the city of Cholet (Maine-et-Loire). Originally specialized in mass-market clothing and shoes – industries that are in decline – the Choletais performed its reconversion by integrating high-end technology to a traditional industry, where governmental plans to group companies together and make them into "global scale businesses" had failed. This was made possible by the quality of its social capital, of its territorial ecosystem that constitutes an "innovative environment" made of solidary relations between economic actors and policies relying on traditional social Christianism, which stimulates synergies between companies, towns, rural workshops and training devices.

This bottom-up approach succeeded when the State's top-down approaches failed. Another example of successful reconversion, the Swiss watchmaking industry used the dynamic of its territory and its social capital to help it resist the offensive of the digital watch by integrating digital technology in high-end watch design.

The scale of the problem posed by monotowns excludes the possibility of assistance policies, a fact that is exacerbated by a restricted budgetary context and the current climate of social and political urgency. It requires a split with the current city design that places the resident at the center – thus the increasing interest in Russia for its history of the *Vetche* and a rediscovery of bottom-up dynamics of endogenous growth that was entirely absent under Soviet rule, completely absorbed with Western scientism. New abilities, design rules need to be developed at the level of central administrations, local governments and for operators. France and Russia are therefore undertaking certain initiatives.

5.3. The worksites of the smart city

The experiences presented above have a common point in that they combine a top-down initiative from the center and the search for a bottom-up dynamic coming from the field, entrenched in the social capital of a smart territory. They differ from experiments in the smart city generally presented in the West that rely on heavy investments in information technologies, where "citizen participation" is generally but a cosmetic role, the human cherry on a cybernetic machine cake.

It is in the light of this approach that we will examine the problems that occur in the transition towards smart cities: transitions in energy, transport, waste and then the new tools that can be used by these approaches.

5.3.1. *The power of data*

Philippe Albrecht, a consultant and researcher, is an ace in data management, but not a geek hoping to build a paradise playing on his keyboard. Data are dangerous to manipulate, because it is playing with the peoples' private lives and even their freedom. In his approach, he uses only data processing – Big Data – to control city management. This is not only to improve management, but also to predict certain events. This is a risky area, where gurus, often more powerful than Erik Schmitt, the CEO of Google, have perfectly understood that whoever controls the data controls the world. How can we develop a practice that does not infringe upon personal liberties and is limited to ends that are good for everyone?

5.3.1.1. *Big Data and smart cities are intrinsically linked*

Big Data is a catch-all term that can be compared to a four-stage rocket: data generation – capture and storage of data – data analysis – governance and optimization.

5.3.1.1.1. The 3Vs: Volume – Velocity – Variety, or the endless increase in data volume

The first stage of the Big Data rocket is exponential and quasi-endless generation of data by all manner of sensors that span all urban activities: energy consumption sensors (smart sensors, among others), energy production sensors and motion sensors – static sensors (cameras – railways) and dynamic sensors – in vehicles – smartphones. These incessant interactions, between men and machine – human to machine (HtM) – between machines – machine to machine (MtM) – are the main vector for this growth. The Big Data adventure is only just beginning: volumes will still be growing from the transformations in digital technologies and their new uses. The energy transitions, for example, will generate new applications that will increase complexity. Energies said to be sustainable (wind turbines, photovoltaic, biomass) in that they are intermittent can only operate when connected as a grid – a meshed relay of production networks – produce vast quantities of data. Amazon now makes most of its revenue from data-hosting than from online retail, and due to the energy cost of transferring data, it does it... with freight trucks. The snowmobile can transport 100 petabytes of data in complete security, and has armed guards!

Figure 5.11. *Amazon snowmobile to transport up to 100 petabytes to the cloud*

The emergence of new roles for a population who are no longer just data-consumers, but also now producers through the use of networks such as smartphones, new consumption habits traceable with dematerialized payments and a finer mesh of territory networks by surveillance systems contributes to this continuous increase in the volume of data.

On top of quantity, there is variety in the sources, therefore new types of consumption such as electric vehicles, new types of charging stations in parking lots, garages and streets. In home automation, the IoT includes all connected household items, sensors (thermostat, smoke alarm, motion sensors, etc.). The data resulting from these objects are both more varied and more precise. They present data about consumption and volume production of fluids, energy, water and prime resources through time. Collecting flows from different networks now occurs in smaller and smaller timeframes and in practically real-time. Counting data is also diversifying: weather, typology of equipment, cartography, recorded alarms, etc.

5.3.1.1.2. Digital technology as a foundation

The second stage relies on digital. This broader, more complex, dense and faster information must be captured, stored and transported to be analyzed and governed. This is where the Internet of Things (IoT) is completed by the digital evolution and innovation. These growing volumes need to be stored and shared. Moore's law is continually being verified[16]. Data are stored on increasingly powerful servers. It is moved around and shared via Cloud Computing that bridges the gap between storage and networks (the Internet, primarily).

The IoT is the backbone of the system

The Internet is the backbone of the massive exchanges of data that are produced and exchanged every second, every nano-second. In 2015, mankind produced as much data in a year as it had in all of history. Today, the total volume of data produced every 12 months doubles. Soon this will be the case every 12 hours. Very soon, we will count 3.4 connected devices per person. The IP (Internet Protocol) traffic will grow 22% every year

---

16 Gordon Moore explained on April 19, 1965 [MOO 65] that digital might grow exponentially. This is the law that made him famous: the power of integrated circuits double, at a constant cost every 18 months.

between 2015 and 2020. This growth is primarily due to MtM (Machine to Machine), which will increase 44% per year between now and 2020 with 50 billion connected objects in the world, 40% of data on the Internet are now produced by connected objects. Three billion people will own smartphones; the whole market representing seven trillion dollars (associated objects and services). According to a recent survey, 84% of people in France stated that connected objects were a source of progress[17]. The Internet has therefore entered the physical realm. It is therefore no longer just an additional layer of the urban system **but its very essence**.

The digital industry is supposed to optimize our consumption of energy, **yet so far it is on its way to posing even more problems of its own, but of a different nature than fossil fuels**. In 2016, 1.5 billion smartphones were sold in the world. To achieve this, the industry used up to 12% of the world's demand for gold, 30% of silver, 30% of copper and up to 80% of rare metals such as ruthenium or indium, the extraction and refining of which cause important environmental damage. Every hour, 10 billion emails are sent, which corresponds to 50 gigawatts of electricity, or the equivalent to 4,000 round trips between Paris and New York on a plane [JAR 17]. 750 billion mobile phones are thrown away each year, along with the highly toxic components inside them such as cadmium, lead, cyanide and mercury that are then sent to China, India and Africa[18]. In France, the data centers that process Big Data have used 10% of the electric energy produced. Digital networks and data processing are undoubtedly part of the solution to the problem of smart cities, but they are also part of a new problem.

5.3.1.1.3. Analysis and optimization

These two first stages are of interest only because they allow us through analysis and governance to accompany the evolution of the city towards optimization. Analysis and assessment are the third stage of Big Data. The importance of data in smart cities effectively find their meaning here. The logic of networks, collecting and processing information, and assessing and measuring their potential and their limits conditions the performance of these cities.

---

17 Agrion and CGI consulting white paper, 2015.
18 See the documentary by Cosima Dannoritzer, *La tragédie électronique*.

Produce useful results for operational teams (professions or IT management: management, networks, customer base, asset management, etc.) by offering massive data analysis capabilities

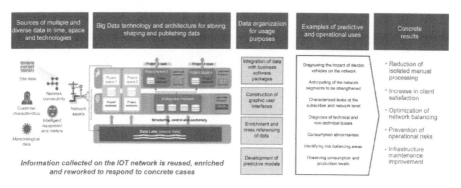

Figure 5.12. *Architecture of Big Data at a major electricity distributor, from analysis to prediction. For a color version of this figure, see www.iste.co.uk/rochet/cities.zip*

The interoperability of these data is at the heart of this analysis. Philippe Albrecht develops the tools that allow him to visualize and understand the operation and consumption of cities and distinguish the dysfunctions and extract from this information the needs for which we should be finding smart services and uses. Figure 5.12 shows how an electric relay manager that manages the accounts of 35 millions users collects data from a multitude of sources in order to predict events and optimize the network. Since July 2013, the fire department of the city of New York has implemented an algorithm that analyzes 60 fire-hazard risk factors [DWO 14]. The level of poverty in the neighborhood, the age of the building, the state of the electrical installation and the presence of automatic fire extinguishing devices are all part of the criteria studied. Similarly, a building that is vacant or unguarded has double the risk of catching fire. The 341 fire units in the city must inspect a total of 50,000 buildings every year. The algorithm in place establishes a risk score for 330,000 buildings and provides a list of priorities that helps the firemen during their weekly inspections that occur depending on the risks identified.

The conditions for success lie in the interoperability of data, that is, access and sharing of data via standard formats (including APIs[19]). The issue

---

19 API stands for *Applications Programming Interface*. An API is a programming interface that helps "plug" into an application to exchange data. An API is open and offered by the program's developer.

involves making data available in a format that is legible and usable for operators, which supposes building a dictionary of data to give them the same format, and a syntax, or grammar that will define how to process them. Thus, the appearance of a new position, which will be critical for tomorrow's cities: Chief Data Officer. Will the control of data be granted to machines or to a company or to the city? Behind this technical conundrum, lies a political challenge.

This issue will grow in relevance with one of the big technological breakthroughs that will help extract the quintessence of Big Data, which is the development of **Artificial Intelligence**. The latter has the capacity to perform analyses and draw conclusions via large-scale algorithms. Machine learning goes even further allowing for self-teaching via the recognition of recurring models (or patterns) and increasing the depth and quality of its optimization.

The stakes for cities are colossal

Let us take the example of the operation of public operators in cities – waste and sewage management, maintaining equipment in working conditions, planning the activities of municipal agents, maintaining parks, etc. According to a study by Mckinsey dating back to 2013, one trillion dollars in savings can be achieved in cities worldwide by optimizing public infrastructures. In fact, the investment towards responding to urban growth between now and 2030 is estimated at 57 trillion dollars[20]. We understand that, over the next 10 years, we could be spending 10 trillion of that amount, while optimizing the city's operation as well as its efficiency and adaptability. To understand the magnitude of these numbers, let us remind readers that the global GDP is somewhere between 100 and 150 trillion dollars, depending on how it is counted (source IMF). Look at water, for instance. In 2013, 60% of domestic water use was in cities. Yet, 14 billion dollars a year are lost due to water leaks or wrong billing. Another essential element of the city is transportation: humans cover a little over 30 billion miles per year to date. It is expected for this number to exceed 150 billion in 2050. At the same time, it is estimated that drivers spend 50 hours a year on average due to delays from congestion in cities.

---

20 See Chapter 2.

Artificial Intelligence would be a major rupture

AI will allow us to precisely identify these malfunctions and take rapid adjustment measures. We can cite, for example, the French electricity provider Enedis that has fitted its network with IoT sensors to analyze dysfunctions on the network and optimize interventions (Figure 5.5). In the case of optimizing transportation in the city, we can look at Waze that is an app that indicates to drivers the optimal route depending on traffic density. This density is calculated primarily thanks to human interaction. Drivers indicate ongoing events on their trip and the algorithm calculates optimal routes in real time.

5.3.1.1.4. Decision-making and governance: distinguishing between short term and long term

The last stage of the rocket is decision-making. Here we must separate immediate operational decision-making, or in other words, how we can influence and govern in real-time and semi real-time (the example of Waze or Enedis) the decision to invest or to plan, which have long-term consequences.

Real-time governance and fundamental split

AI applies well to operational governance, because it relies on the analysis of repeating processes and behaviors. Thanks to Big Data, the city can be governed to manage permanent optimizations: balancing traffic, energy consumption and production. In cities and territories that function or that will function on the same objects on multi-energy and multi-materials, where production is increasingly decentralized, the ability to permanently adjust towards the equilibrium between supply and demand will provide phenomenal performance gains (as explained above). For the first time on a volume and complexity scale that currently has a seemingly endless potential for growth, we are seeing the appearance of a permanent feedback loop between bottom-up (information going upwards) and top-down (decision going downwards). The datum (and therefore the machine) governs our reality.

Luis Bettencourt tells us the story of the unexpected discovery he made during a conference at CalTech (California Institute of Technology) [BET 13b]: attending a conference on connected vehicles, he spoke up to highlight the importance of taking into account the human factor. "No need", answered the CalTech researchers. The problem with human decision-making is that it occurs in timeframes in the order of the second whereas machines operate on feedback (the time between perceiving a situation and taking action) that is in the order of the millisecond. It is therefore more reliable to let the machine handle situations as long as the situation encountered is supported by the system. Under certain conditions, concludes Luis Bettencourt, you do not need to be very smart because simple automated situations can solve very difficult problems. In certain situations, as long as all the parameters are integrated into the model, which is *de facto* impossible outside of a controlled environment, human vigilance will no longer be required.

Long-term decisions can be optimized by predictive systems

Long-term decisions, however, mean imagining, trying, testing and adjusting. AI is no longer enough in this space and human intelligence is predominant. Predictive models help seek efficiency (the result) and effectiveness (the means used) of private, public and mixed economic decision-making. They respond to fixed objectives that can be qualified as optimal, keeping in mind that these optimums are inherently temporary and do not represent an optimal equilibrium. For example, if we look at the perspective of public decision-making in the service of the city, the following optimums could be created:

– development of the economy and employment;

– increase in fluidity of mobility;

– optimization of energy consumption;

– response to population increases or dips;

– transition towards new economic models, etc.;

– the starting or mature state of what already exists;

– restrictions, financial ones, for example (investment capacity, indebtment, balance between l'OPEX/CAPEX, etc.).

Visualization tools facilitate decision-making

Lastly, visualization tools are the final layer that help facilitate decision-making ergonomics. PRECARITAIR (Figure 5.6), developed for EDF, helps target areas of energetic poverty and target the impact of tariff variations over the solvability of populations. This tool also helps orient renovation and isolation policies of buildings in order for it to profit the poorest.

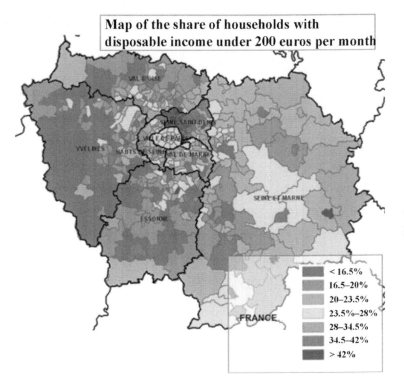

Figure 5.13. *EDF's tool PRECARITAIR helps visualize energy poverty-prone areas*

Mass data processing therefore allows predictive action at a low cost both in terms of operation and more importantly in terms of impact over society. Big Data will therefore be of great help towards understanding the dynamics of dissipative systems (human systems) that are not accessible to the laws of physics. Data processing will help understand in broad strokes how a social system behaves, how a human system behaves, a city, a neighborhood, and those broad strokes understandings will be enough to act on a system's dynamic.

Philippe Albrecht develops tools that will allow us to visualize and understand a city's consumption, its operation, as well as discern any dysfunctions and outline from this information whatever needs should be addressed with smart services. He has taken the initiative of providing a new angle to the discipline, a frugal one, using the best aspects of OPEN DATA and OPEN SOURCE.

5.3.1.2. *From open data to predictive data*

Open data is the public counterpart of Open Source. It is information made available to all for free use. It is a common good. Public open data is spreading rapidly in France, under the impetus of the INSEE that makes a large amount of data available to the public, the precision and the value of which are highly underestimated. For example, the electricity billing regulatory law (or TURPE) insists on the goal of transparency towards operators in this sector, that user-data pertains to the consumption and transport of electricity be made available on open-access platforms.

5.3.1.2.1. The knowledge of wealth comes from cross-data referencing

Companies have started pooling together their data on specific subjects, knowing that sharing this information will be more beneficial than keeping it to themselves. Take a look at the example of the Avere-France, an association that gathers all industrial, commercial and institutional stakeholders in electric mobility: manufacturers, distributors and maintenance professionals; equipment fabricators, energy experts, installers for batteries, charging systems, components, etc.

On this basis, Philippe Albrecht and his company PCG have created an innovative application based on a simple idea: placing oneself in the shoes of a sporting equipment vendor. It relies on three sources of information: *static data* of *open data* that provides a distribution of population based on their age, profession and family status. *Dynamic data*, collected from smartphones, credit cards and all other sources, and lastly, *predictive data* that are the result of cross-referencing the data from the two previous sources. The quality of predictive data improves over each predictive cycle and can tell us how people get to the gym, allowing businesses to place billboards and advertising materials on their route. If, on top of this, we can find out at what times they will go past this billboard, and on which days, targeting can be even better. Thanks to Open Data, we have catalogs of products and their prices, and we are then capable of valuing the route. Philippe Albrecht's teams have developed a product – SPOOK (see

Figure 5.14) – that helps favor the potential revenue that can be made on the different routes depending on the product we want to sell.

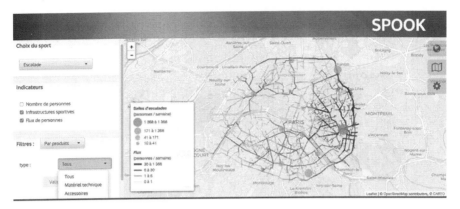

Figure 5.14. *Predictive data applied to identifying the value of people's movements in Paris depending on their ability to buy climbing equipment*

In the screenshot above, we can see the value of people's movements in Paris depending on their ability to buy climbing equipment. The points represent sporting installations. The thickness of the line represents its value and, in this case, the purchasing potential. We can see the potential that this app can provide, if we want to manage other types of activities like security around stadiums, channel flows of supporters during large sporting events. Collectives manage tourist flows on tourist sites from data gathered from smartphones that give their nationalities and tell them how they move around. Static data of *open data* provide statistics on tourism habits, in a way that their trips can be improved. From *open data*, we can develop territorial nano-targeting to target precisely, to within a street, the value of a geographic point, depending on who uses it, where they are coming from and where they are going. From Big Data to big brother.

We can never talk about Big Data without touching on cybersecurity, something that is now a full-on discipline of the smart city. From security and confidentiality of data and the political independence of a city, the stakes are considerable.

The Snowden case showed us how a government can surveil its citizens with considerable means, in this instance, the NSA (National Security Agency). Under the direction of General Keith Alexander from 2005 to

2014, the agency decided to "collect everything", including digital communications, to know everything about everyone, in the name of national security, obviously. These practices were revealed to the world by Edward Snowden, who was subsequently forced to leave the USA, along with journalist Glenn Greenwald, who gave a detailed account of the NSA's practices [GRE 14]. The NSA made confidential agreements with major social networks and search engines to access their data. It adds its sources to the control of digital traffic on communications networks to intercept emails, any phone communication, anything going through a wired connection. This was called the PRISM program (Figure 5.15): everything is intercepted, analyzed by powerful machines capable of drawing links between data that are meaningless by themselves. In principle, the access to messages is protected, but not the access to the metadata. For example, a machine will detect that Mrs. X called her lab to receive the results of a test, then Planned Parenthood, then a man who is not her husband. We can immediately detect an affair and a critical situation that can give an opportunity for blackmail.

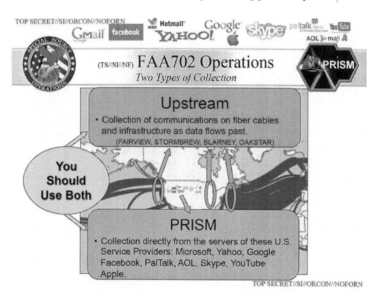

Figure 5.15. *Top secret presentation of the PRISM data interception program by the NSA, revealed by Edward Snowden (source: Glenn Greenwald)*

The NSA, FBI, CIA and even the DoJ (Department of Justice) work together to achieve political objectives for the US government, and will share data with corporations when their interests are at stake. This is used in an example of American extraterritorial law. An email passing through a server located on American soil was enough to grant the DoJ the ability to investigate the activities of said company and subject it to an investigation under anti-corruption laws and have access to all of its data. This is how GE took possession of Alstom[21].

A cold war is ongoing on digital networks. The United States are working in close proximity with Canada, Australia, New Zealand, the UK and have close partnerships with twenty other countries. On the other side, the Russians and the Chinese are developing their own strategies.

It is not just about intercepting data: the NSA can implant malwares on any device and control how its owner uses it, by reading keystrokes, or even infect it with a virus that will block the information system. Digital security is therefore a considerable issue when talking about resilient cities. Cities often do not have the necessary abilities to undo all of these traps and build cyber-security systems, which requires collaborating with central agencies, such as the ANSSI (*Agence nationale pour la Sécurité des Systèmes d'Information* [National Agency for the Safety of Information Systems]) in France.

5.3.2. *How much do smart cities cost?*

We saw in Chapter 4 the case made by the American Association of Civil Engineers on the cost of obsolete infrastructures in the USA and the benefit that stem from modernizing them. Their costs, from then on, are no longer costs but rather investments, as long as we account for derivative impacts, the positive and negative externalities. We saw in Chapter 4 how the American Association of Civil Engineers calculated the cost of obsolete infrastructures and the impact of renovating them, which surpasses the costs by far. Those costs then immediately become investments that add value. For Phil Banes, Director of *smart city council*, a group of producers that consult for cities on their investments, *smart cities won't cost anything* if investments on digital technology are performed wisely by integrating technological building blocks during large urban renovation projects.

In the externalities, there is not only the cost of obsolete infrastructures, but there are also other externalities such as pollution, stress, energy and

---

21 Regarding American extraterritorial stategies, see [ROC 16b].

waste. We know that the larger the city, the more the waste, pollution and stress it produces and that its energy consumption grows proportionally to its size.

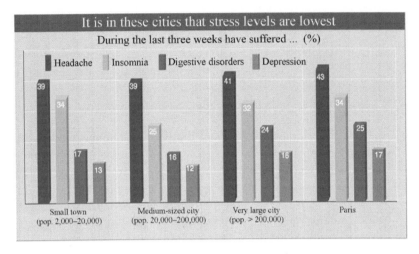

Figure 5.16. *Growth of stress according to the size of a city [MAR 98] (source: INRA-CREDOC 1998). For a color version of this figure, see www.iste.co.uk/rochet/cities.zip*

Figure 5.16 shows the relationship between a city's size and the growth in stress and their derivative ailments. We find here the conclusions of Paul Bairoch on the optimal size of a city being below 200,000 habitants. In Mexico Ciudad, where there are 21 million people, the average time spent in public transport is four hours, supposing that 10 million people are commuting, which makes a combined 40 million hours wasted every single day. These hours can be converted to work not being done, pollution, stress and less time with family. This spoilage of social life is inevitably reflected in crime stats throughout the city.

As early as 1920, British economist A.C. Pigou suggested taking into account externalities into cost calculation. This is desirable as long as we can establish a city's accurate total costs.

Let us look at the example of waste: in 1925, economist Stuart Chase described the phenomenon in *The Tragedy of Waste*, not only from a economics perspective, but by questioning a number of social sciences that were outside the production sphere and that needed to be accounted for beyond direct costs in terms of wasted time, wasted produce and quality of life, in a way that reflected the inter-relations between products and waste. Waste production was at the heart of the production model during the second industrial revolution. In 1924, the Phoebus cartel, an oligopoly uniting incandescent light bulb manufacturers, launched the idea of *programmed obsolescence* effectively shortening the lifespan of their bulbs from 2,500 to 1,000 hours. Oil companies along with Renault in France, General Motors in the United States, torpedoed electric street car systems in order to replace them with buses. Waste production was becoming the key to the economy denounced by Kenneth Galbraith in *The Affluent Society* [GAL 58]). Limitless urban expansion in the USA, analyzed by Lewis Mumford, becomes a black hole of consumption of automobiles, energy and pollutant products. With globalization, it is a more insidious form of waste management that settles in accordance with the theory of Lawrence Summers, according to which it is more rational to pollute poor countries than rich ones.

China became the most polluting country because it based its growth on becoming the northern world's workshop. Today's tragedy of waste is in dissociation with areas of production – in poor countries – and consumption – in rich countries. The sincerity of costs command that negative externalities generated in poor countries be taken into account.

In the case of digital, that we present a technology that is fundamental to solving these problems, which is in turn seen as clean technology with its white rooms and its immaterial aspect, the situation is even worse. Producing digital technologies is consuming rare earth minerals, which require a lot of pollution to produce. Bernard Tourillon, director of Uragold, a company that produces materials for solar energy, estimates that the production of a solar panel for an individual generates 70 kilos of CO_2. Are electric cars the solution? Building one of them requires far more energy than a fossil fuel automobile due to the weight of lithium ion batteries [NEA 15].

Journalist Guillaume Pitron wrote an article about the production of rare earth minerals that demonstrate their prohibitive costs and the catastrophic impact of their use [PIT 18]. China has renewed its rare earth mineral strategy of sub-contracting waste from the West. Not only does this allow rich countries to pollute without care, but it also allows them not to have to think about how rare earth mineral waste is recycled, an operation that is difficult and costly, meaning that only 10% of rare metals are recycled today. Green cities thanks to digital technology? A considerable increase in pollution and the production of waste above all else.

Transport is at the source of considerable external costs. In France, the ADEME assesses the drop in life expectancy linked to exposure to fine particles to be of 8.2 months. According to the OMS, pollution due to particles is the cause of on average 6% of premature deaths in France, half of which are attributed to traffic emissions. The latest scientific studies reinforce this link between pollution in the air and breathing and cardiovascular diseases and evidence effects on our ability to reproduce, as well as fetal and neurological development. Nitrous oxide (NO_2) and ozone (O_3) also prove to be toxic for humans and to have negative effects on our ecosystems. The health costs (premature deaths, chronic bronchitis, etc.) of pollution represent each year between 20 and 30 billion euros in France. Add to this, the cost of wasted time and of stress.

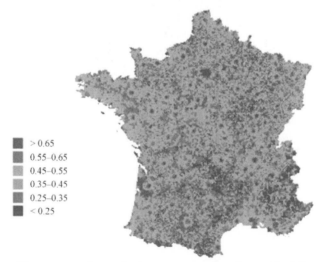

> 0.65
0.55–0.65
0.45–0.55
0.35–0.45
0.25–0.35
< 0.25

Home–work emissions per active household
(CO_2 / household . year)

Figure 5.17. *Pollution emissions linked to commuting between home and workplace, measured per household (source: Energie demain)*

Electric vehicles may appear at first glance as a solution, as they emit only 32 tons of carbon from factory to scrapyard, which is half of what a petrol car would. However, its production consumes three to four times more energy. Overall, throughout the car's entire lifecycle, an electric car produces three quarters of the pollution of its petrol equivalent, and this is when talking about a car that must be recharged every 120 km. With Tesla announcing that their cars have an autonomy of 800 km, the advantage of electric cars are going to decrease even further. Texan lawyer John Petersen, is quoted by Guillaume Pitron, who has built a career in the battery industry as concluding "electric vehicles are technically possible, but their production will never be sustainable from an environmental point of view", which is the same conclusion reached by the ADEME "over the course of its lifecycle, the energy consumption of an electric car is overall the same as that of a diesel" [ADE 16].

Here, though, all externalities must be included in the costs. Where does the electricity come from? What will be the impact of recycling a large park of electric vehicles? Is a city that forbids automotive circulation in its city center just "shoveling snow into the neighbor's yard[22]"? Calculations performed by the research center *Energie demain* highlight the location of the source of the pollution linked to commuting (Figure 5.17): French city centers may appear green, but this is only because pollution is moved to the outskirts. We have seen the impact of gentrification phenomena on housing prices in city centers, to make room for the "creative classes" and their cycling lanes.

In Paris, it is forbidden to drive along the banks of the Seine. This translates to an increase in pollution, in particular along the highways around Paris, on the Eastern side, in the lower income suburbs. Drivers using the river banks are mostly crossing through the city and do not actually live there. In exchange for a minimal decrease in pollution in the immediate vicinity, the Airparif association [AIR 17] has found that we are seeing a high increase in pollution all the way along the traffic veins (Figure 5.9).

This is an expression of a law of architecture of complex systems: over-optimizing a function leads to under-optimizing the overall system. Building pedestrian streets will have an impact on the direct environment, but if we want to gauge the global impact, we need to look at the impact on the overall circulation flows.

---

22 A Quebec saying.

What is the conclusion? There is currently no golden bullet for ending pollution. Common decency says that we have to account for exported pollution linked to production. There are nascent technologies that would help produce in more eco-friendly manners, such as small modular reactors that can be developed in short amounts of time and produce 300 MGW, which is enough to power a small town and its outskirts, and with a waste production of 4% of that of a classic reactor, and a short lifespan, and almost no waste in the case of thorium reactors. Smart cities remain in all aspects fodder for innovation.

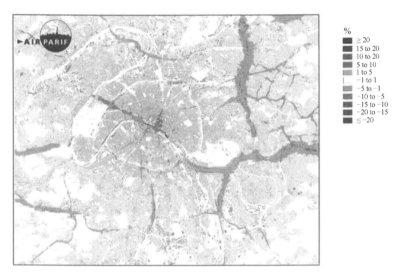

Figure 5.18. *Effect of moving pollution away due to traffic being pushed towards the outskirts because of river banks being closed off in Paris (source: Airparif)*

The cheapest and least polluting energy is the one we do not use. We can act to reduce the transportation time and therefore the pollution that goes with it, as in the case of commutes. They grow proportionally to the size of the city, in the urban Parisian area; it is the order of 70 minutes (Figure 5.19). Beyond 1 h of transportation, fatigue can be felt and impacts working conditions. Note that fatigue is mostly experienced by people using public transport [MIN 15].

Reducing time spent in transport can be done in many different ways. The first is to control the price of housing in city centers that is shooting up under the effect of transport networks. In NYC, all networks converge towards Manhattan, which contributes to skyrocketing prices. This is the case in Paris as well, where prices are linked to proximity to transports. Gentrification policies that led to the working classes being driven out to the outskirts contribute directly to increasing transport times, as well as the suburbanization phenomenon, which leads executives to look for houses with gardens outside the city at the cost of a longer commute. As was suggested by urban designer Jan Gehl, the key is therefore to control the housing prices by starting with property prices. In tourism-driven towns like Chamonix, property prices have increased so much that the city can no longer afford to host the personnel it needs to operate the tourist installations, which then contributes to the increase in circulation in the *haute vallée de l'Arve*.

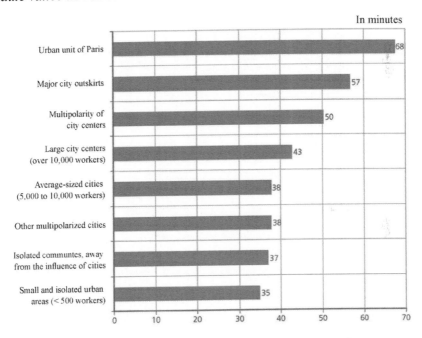

Figure 5.19. *Commute time according to the size of the city (source: DARES analyses, November 2015)*

The other element is work organization. The photo in Figure 5.20 presents the corridors of the French Ministry of Finance during the middle of the work day. Every employee is in their own office, with no contact with other employees outside of the lunch break, for those who eat together. Offices are organized linearly along long anonymous corridors. The neo-Stalinist architecture of this ministry reflect the work organization of the second industrial revolution; one that values mass production and requires standardized isolated tasks and a central production of energy that means aligning work stations and no communication between employees. In his patterns, Christopher Alexander had already identified the possibility of distributing work in a variety of locations, something that is all the more possible in the age of digital. This is different to teleworking, which would not solve the problem of worker isolation and would not respond to security standards for the tasks in question, but rather to design communicative workplaces.

Figure 5.20. *The corridors of the Ministry of Finance in Paris during the middle of the day: each employee works in their own office without any interaction with others*

In conclusion, any architectural and urban planning decision involves costs in terms of transport, energy, pollution, waste recycling, stress, public health as well as increased synergies that they encourage. Reasoning in complete costs that integrate the externalities, an idea started by A.C. Pigou in 1920, will be a necessity when public management undergoes its inevitable restructure.

5.3.3. *The government of a smart city*

As early as 1613, Neapolitan Antonio Serra, in a memoir presented to the Vice-Roy of Naples, *"on the causes that allow an abundance of gold and silver in kingdoms that do not have mines"*[23] maintains that there are activities that are more productive than others and formulates the principle of increasing returns in the industry, linked to the development and freedom of cities. Serra is in fact the first to have formulated the principles of an "industrial policy", where the state directs the economy towards activities with higher added value, following the principles of cumulative effects relating to learning, something that the theory evolution will reuse under the concept of "technological path" trajectory phenomenon. Serra ended up in prison, his work being considered irreverent by the Viceroy – and Southern Italy remained feudal and never followed the route of industrialization that the North did with its flourishing cities.

Economic development is linked with the harmony of urban life, where economic activities can enter in synergy and where the dynamic equilibrium and the evolution of the city are ensured by a government driven by the ideal of common good and classic wisdom as represented in the murals by Ambroggio Lorenzetti on the town hall in Sienna (Figure 3.2). The increasing complexity of cities, their dysfunctional developments and the predominance of top-down urban planning have made us forget these strong principles. In an analysis of ongoing smart city initiatives, Italian researchers united around Paolo Neirotti of Torino's Politecnico [NEI 14] found that there is none that embraces all fields, physical domains, transports, natural resources and energy. The city's government and administration will not necessarily be a smart system of life. In fact, teo models emerge from the Neirotti study, one is technocentric, heavily pushed by technology vendors, and the other based on the people, but the technocentric is dominant.

The problem is that the technocentric approach is upheld by corporations with efficient marketing strategies that, unfortunately, work. In addition,

---

23 Antonio Serra's forefront role as an economist of industrial development and cities was proposed by Erik Reinert and especially by his son Sophus, professor at Harvard [REI 16].

there are no vendors of good governing, quality of life and civic life; this is an issue because the systemic integration of the city relies on this ability for people to appropriate technological systems and make them serve their purposes. The social capital is the inevitable base on which the technical capital must take root if it is to truly contribute to the emergence of an urban intelligence.

One of the remaining tasks to undertake is to grant our political figures a practical and methodological baggage for integrating these two types of domain.

5.3.4. *What are the tasks and what is the form of a smart government for a smart city?*

A city is first and foremost a place where economic opportunities are created. This occurs through synergies between activities, and therefore between people. Public policies can favor – or block – the conditions for their creation. They develop naturally when civic life is active. The rise of the digital sphere has meant that people must be vigilant to ensure the validity of an investment, assess local and foreign pollution, and demand transparency to avoid corruption. These are subject truths presented as established or imperative to public debate. Digital opens new fields to innovation and a new role to the user that must be favored for two reasons: creativity and validating social utility and innovation. We have demonstrated abundantly that smart cities are political projects above being technical ones. Experiences past and ongoing show the importance of popular participation, which makes direct democracy a viable government model.

5.3.4.1. *Searching for synergies between economic activities*

The ideal-type smart city can refer to the model imagined by Thünen, a center where interactions are high, surrounded by concentric areas that move towards less and less increasing returns, from food crops to extensive agriculture, from the specialized industrial areas to dispersed activities. The task of public policies is to look for synergies between activities with strong increasing returns and not the accumulation of ultramodern technologies. The town of Loos-en-Gohelle, a town suffering from the ancient mining basin, is reinventing itself around a sustainable territorial project. It is a life project that relies on the principle of frugal innovation. The new initiatives have been led with a two-pronged objective, of breaking away from the current model and proceeding in "baby steps". This is how the method of eco-construction was developed for social housing and municipal buildings. Or even new operative models pertaining to urbanism, the environment (infiltration lines, *ceinture verte*, varying management of green areas, etc.). At first performed on a "case by case" basis, these actions have little by little begun to define a coherent frame: as they have developed they have highlighted bridges between different fields of intervention, introducing a form of transversality in managing the commune. It is an emergent innovation model that integrates external technological advances [ROC 08].

5.3.4.2. *Supporting open innovation*

In contemporary smart cities, digital technologies grant residents more power to use and produce information, but also applications. The experiences of cities that have opened their data to the public have found that the feedback from these bottom-up approaches tend to pay off. In Washington DC, Anthony Townsend [TOW 13] explains that an "app for democracy" contest was organized with the aim to encourage developers to create apps from public resources. For an investment of 50,000 $ the return was very quick with 47 applications developed in 30 days and a combined value of two million dollars, or a 4,000% return for the city. However, this should not be an indication that bottom-up approaches are a universal solution. Most of these applications were in their 1.0 versions and untested with no user feedback and, of course, unsecured. They were developed by *techies* fascinated by the technology and used to "making something", without that something ever being validated, whereas a city will need apps that have gone through all of those validation and testing phases.

We are rediscovering here one of the laws of innovation put forward by Eric von Hippel [VON 86]: the key role of lead users in the innovation process, they are the first to adopt an innovation and *de facto* take part in the innovation process. This has, in fact, always been a trait of the innovation process, even though it was somewhat forgotten during the industrial era, as François Caron reminds us in his works on history of innovation [CAR 12].

Institutions can greatly support this innovation process. National innovation [FRE 95] systems provide a context that incites cooperation between industries, research and investors to direct their activities towards risk-taking innovations. However, the administration's ability to control systems would be greatly favored by development of an *extended administration* able to embrace the perimeter of innovation and therefore guarantee that this innovation and the applications that result from it are focused on the real needs of the people of the city.

Journalist Bénédicte Manier explains that these apps are very inventive on a number of endogenous innovations that she encountered, the "million peaceful revolutions" that were the subject of a book she wrote [MAN 13]. She catalogs a multitude of actions emerging from small groups in society, where the emphasis is placed on favoring all things local and community self-management. Fields of application are multiple and pertain to water management, cooperative businesses, localized distribution and consumption models, currency-less exchanges, local currencies or socially responsible banks, agricultural experiments in urban environments, sustainable farming, attempts at local autonomy in terms of energy, solidary residents' "citizen health-centers", and territorial management where citizens and political entities collaborate.

5.3.4.3. *An active civic life*

Political philosophy was born in Greece with cities and urban civilization. The most insightful and relevant analyst on what makes a city great was Machiavelli who emphasized the role of common good: "*...It's not the particular good but the common good that makes cities great. Common good is not observed if not in republics*" writing in one of his discourses on the first decade of Titus Livius. Machiavelli imagined common good as part of the philosophical tradition of Thomas Aquinas as something more than the sum of its parts. The systemic equilibrium of this entity is permanently in question by the corruptive force of *fortuna* – chance, generator of *corruptio* (which is not material corruption, but the collective loss of virtue), which must constantly be compensated by the Prince's *virtù*, this combination of force (*vir*) and virtue (*virtus*) which must be the fundamental characteristic of a public leader.

Public management has an inherently systemic nature. When the social system is subject to multiple events, it becomes highly entropic and needs to create negentropy thanks to the connections between the members of the city that is created by *vivere politico* in Machiavelli's book, or the civic life, which organizes the equilibrium between power of a large number of citizens and the small number of powerful leaders who tend to accumulate power in the city [ROC 10]. Civic life is a necessary space of controversies that allow institutions to evolve. A conservative historian, François Guizot, attributed the success of European civilization to class struggles[24], in that it helped build compromises and allowed institutions to evolve, on condition no class ever won. In contemporary complex societies, Elinor and Vincent Ostrom [OST 10] have developed the concept of polycentric governance, which is organized on two axes, one descendant according to each level of social organization complexity, and the other horizontal between the organizations. It is essential that there are areas that overlap between the organizations of the city: the excess of rationality that creates rigid boundaries between organizations and missions does not correspond to real life and inhibits innovations and the necessary characterization of public institutions.

5.3.4.4. *Direct democracy, the best regime for a smart city?*

Political philosophy ponders which would be the best regime for a city. Many options have been debated throughout the centuries: the first being to have a government composed of the best citizens, the *aristoï*, or aristocrats. There was logic to this solution – aristocrats are supposed to have the time available and education level to take care of the city and be subject to govern for the common good and not for their own welfare – but it was never confirmed. Machiavelli said it best: he established that common good is only truly defended in a Republic. The Italian diplomat reached his conclusion following the requisite class struggle that institutions had to organize and regulate, and used the example of the tribunal in Rome, which mediated arguments between the small number of aristocrats (*popolo grasso*) by a great number of people (*popolo minuto*). English and subsequent French revolutions gave way to the representative-based regime, which entrusts representatives to argue on behalf of the people. This form of government

---

24 "Modern Europe, indeed, is born of this struggle between the different classes of society. I have already shown that in other places this struggle has been productive of very different consequences; in Asia, for example, one particular class has completely triumphed, and the system of castes has succeeded that of classes, and society has there fallen into a state of immobility. Nothing of this kind, thank God has taken place in Europe. One of the classes has not conquered, has not brought the others into subjection; no class has been able to overcome, to subjugate the others, the struggle, instead of rendering society stationary, has been a principal cause of its progress, the relations of the different classes with one another; the necessity of combating and of yielding by turns; the variety of interests, passions, and excitements; the desire to conquer without the power to do so: from all this has probably sprung the most energetic, the most productive principle of development in European civilization" [GUI 98].

has all the prerogatives of an aristocracy but must subject itself to the election process and open the "political class" to whoever wishes to enter it.

Pure direct democracy has always existed in smaller communities where all residents can interact, like under the African palaver tree[25], but many mixed forms have always existed, one notorious example being of a mixed form – an oligarchic regime under popular control – was Venice during the urban expansion in the Middle Ages. Jean-Claude Barrea sees this as the birthplace of modern capitalism, capitalism that understood that social harmony and civil right were the most effective conditions to a city's prosperity [BAR 11].

Among the models of direct democracy, random selection was practiced in Ancient Greece and the urban republics of the Renaissance period, with the objective of avoiding "political class" from taking control. King Ferdinand II of Aragon once stated "From experience, we can see that the so-called regimes of drawing lots out of the bag, in cities and towns, favoring the good life, a health administration and a healthy regime more than the regimes that are based, on the other hand, on election" [SIN 11]. Randomly selecting citizens to hold public functions is different from the examples of purely cosmetic "participation" that seems to be the current predominant practice, due to the pitfalls of purely bureaucratic and technical approaches: the idea is to really exercise power. This can be in order to validate a public contract, its opportunity and conditions award, to deliberate on what a city should and should not be, a prerogative that is all the more important in a context where lobbies of all sorts tend to impose their choices as accepted truths. This can be accomplished with a random selection among all citizens, from a list of volunteers or based on a list of aptitudes when technical knowledge is required. It is also essential that this does not become a practice for the "leisure classes", in reference to the works of Thorstein Veblen[26], to avoid this activity becoming exclusive to the "creative classes", and for the former to spend time in "participative debates" reduced to a pointless exchange of platitudes.

---

25 See Chapter 5.

26 Thorstein Veblen [VEB 99], Norwegian-American sociologist and economist, in *the theory of the leisure class* – which in Norwegian translates to something closer to "the theory of people who do nothing" – demonstrated that industrialization had led the world to be controlled by a leisure class that spends its time running after.

One can be a partisan of direct democracy through political conviction that it is the "best regime" or simply for reasons pertaining to the operation of the urban ecosystem [ROC 17b]. In the case of Christchurch, we have seen that the direct power of the people is a condition for the *resilience* of the system, because to face an unexpected event (in this case, an earthquake), the system must be able to generate quick interactions within itself, thus promoting the ability of its people to organize among themselves without relying on the State. Another reason can be the economic prosperity of cities: economic decline is caused by an absence of vitality in the cooperation between residents and companies. A State's collapse is always preceded by an urban collapse, as explained by Erik Reinert and Rainer Kattel [REI 09], and the closer the participation system between residents is to a democracy, the more the growth is focused on education, health and communication infrastructures, the more the inequality decreases and the more the cities and States can regain stability. One last reason that pleads in favor of direct democracy is the technological intensity of a smart city. We saw earlier the role of users in developing products and the threat posed by dominion from large tech corporations and the threats of cybersecurity. The power of corruption of representatives here is considerable and makes it necessary to place these under popular control.

Readers may be surprised about the paradox while mentioning direct democracy in connection with examples such as Singapore, which was created and led with iron will by Lee Kwan Yew. However, Machiavelli tells us that such an institutional system does not appear spontaneously, and that it must be *instituted* by a founding creator[27] who stabilizes institutions. A good Prince is one who gives good institutions that are going to allow the city to organize itself around the common good by giving the "largest number" of people the means to fight the tendencies of the "smallest number" of rich and powerful from acquiring control. A "well established"

---

27 There are self-regulating social systems that appear without an architectural intervention or a founding creator, but this pertains to small communities such as the ones studied by Elinor Ostrom for resource management of water as a common good, where informal collective institutions are created spontaneously. Elinor Ostrom mentions that she only identified this phenomenon in small communities of less than 15,000 people, where regulating transgressions occur immediately due to the swiftness of interactions within the community. This approach is confirmed in institutional economy by the works of Avner Greif, a researcher influenced by the hypothesis of spontaneous order emitted by Friedrich Hayek: when size increases and interactions between actors within the system decrease, the capacity for private interests to generate endogenous rules in social relations decreases.

(*bene ordinata*) republic sets fundamental laws, metarules that will be able to adapt to specific contexts. Machiavelli was the first to imagine this imperative for a sustainable State, which resulted in *two antagonist movements*: the creative action of a prince who can use the routes of a legitimate and energetic authority (*virtù*, a combination of ancient civic virtue (*virtus*) and the founding force of the city (*vir*)) and adaptability. The "perfect republic" in Machiavelli's mind does not proceed from an ideal, timeless vision, but from its capacity to transform along with the mutations that disturb it. Both poles of this tension are the heroic action of the Prince and his *virtù* and the political life that ensures civic participation of the greatest number, the *vivere politico*. It is the paradox of the *benevolent dictator* as he was created under the Roman Republic, which creates the conditions for a Republic and then disappears.

To place this in modern and systemic terms, Machiavelli considers that class struggles are permanent and play a regulatory role for an adaptive system confronted by the entropy generated by randomness and uncertainty, which Machiavelli referred to as *fortuna*. Negentropy is then produced by civic life – *vivere politico* – that allows the system to reach a superior level of equilibrium.

In the case of Singapore, it is the architecture rules for the system that are centralized to maintain its coherence. However, it is in line with the logic of evolution towards an autopoietic system that this regulatory role is progressively ensured by civic behavior, as is the case in Switzerland, for example.

The concept of a smart city, necessarily autopoietic, relies on a contradiction: designing through a ruling founding act, the government of a system that in time will govern itself.

Conclusion

Over one hundred years ago, in reaction to worsening living conditions resulting from the first industrial revolution, the French *mouvement ouvrier* (workers' movement) was launched on May 1, 1906 to fight for the eight-hour working day. This was not only a fight for better working conditions, but for better living conditions that the labor organizations of the time were trying to improve through daily pragmatic actions and by opening the *caisses de secours mutuel* (mutual aid funds), the *bourses du travail* (labor exchange), through popular literature and workers' leisure. The idea was to achieve a better work–life balance for everyone.

Today, we work less than eight hours, but then replace that time with hours of transport and leisures that are often meek in social contact, and sleep that is becoming a pathology linked to the stress of urban life.

A smart city is something between the pursuit of the work of the utopists, beyond Ebenezer Howard in England and the US, with the development of social housing in France that did not resemble the modern uniform and miserable tower blocks that begin to appear in the 1950s. Between 1921 and 1933 in Stains (Seine-Saint-Denis), the *Office public des habitations bon marché du département de la Seine* built a total of 1,640 social housing units, including 480 detached houses, which remains one of the prettiest examples of garden cities. These systems of life – which exist today and present an example for urbanist formations – were the polar opposite of the "machines for living in" that should today be destroyed at great expense to rediscover the charm of the *little* in contrast to our fascination with *big is beautiful* that has hypnotized our elites who revel in the cult of the metropolis.

Figure C.1. *Poster for the workers' protest of 12 May 1906, fighting for the eight-hour day*

A city has always been a political matter; specifically, how to organize life inside a city. Cities have asked – and continue to ask – all of the questions, from the fundamental philosophical questions appearing in Athens on *what is the good life?*, to questions pertaining to what is beauty, the economy, communication, life in society and today, the potential of digital technologies. The latter are not an invitation to forget the past, but rather to use it for inspiration because, as shown by Christoper Alexander, most questions raised by the city today have been asked before in the past. The only difference is that now they are being asked with new tools that provide new possibilities and new problems, which call for us to develop social and technological intelligence.

Making cities smart is an obligatory point of passage in our development to face the challenges of the 21st Century. A spoilt urban development leads to underdevelopment and foreshadows a state's failure. The health of a city gives us an indication of the health of a country, and an unhealthy country allows us to diagnose the failures of the State, which is known as FFF: a *failing, fragile and failed state.*

Not only development imperatives, but also power relations because there is a competition in the realm of designing smart cities as *systems of systems*: whoever masters the rules and the tools, will control subsequent bid solicitations and nascent markets. *Soft power* is already a major driver for sustaining the emergence of a dominant standard.

Designing smart cities is a lever for innovation and endogenous growth in order to create "Gerschenkron-esque" catch-up effects and reshuffle the deck in terms of technological power. We can see this happening with China, which, at the cost of sacrificing its own environment, has caught up with its technological delay in a matter of decades and now captures key resources of the digital economy and is becoming the world's leading research lab for industrial solutions to fighting pollution while implementing clusters of smart cities. The parts of the world with the most failing, polluted and polluting industry, India, China and Africa, will be the world's next great drivers of innovation. Russia seems well positioned to play on the duality between the urgency of its urban renovation and the revitalization of its strategy of innovation to get back up after its dark history during the 20th Century. Latin America, on its way toward stabilization, will offer turnarounds as spectacular as the one in Medellín, innovative experiences such as the *ciudad dulce*, sweet cities in Costa Rica, in symbiosis with their environments.

By emphasizing bottom-up approaches, designing smart cities becomes a process that is more adapted to emerging countries than Western top-down technocentric approaches: promoting local resources, developing social capitals, embracing history, embracing the territory, technological and financial independence, etc.

Beyond this, reading Isabelle Delannoy's beautiful book, we can dream of a *symbiotic economy* that would merge innovations from all fields of production and organization and solve all problems created by over a century's worth of urban decay resulting from a world forgetting history's lessons. An economy of intelligence, what a challenge!

References

[ADE 16] ADEME, Les potentiels du véhicule électrique, Report, April 2016.

[AIR 17] AIRPARIF, Voies sur berges : la qualité de l'air un an après, available at: https://www.airparif.asso.fr/actualite/detail/id/213, 2017.

[ALE 77] ALEXANDER C., ISHIKAWA S., SILVERSTEIN M., *A Pattern Language, Town, Buildings, Constructions*, Oxford University Press, Oxford, 1977.

[ALE 16] ALEXANDER C., *A City is Not a Tree*, Sustasis Press, 2016.

[AUZ 15] AUZANEAU M., *Or Noir*, La Découverte, Paris, 2015.

[AYD 85] AYDALOT P., *Économie Régionale et Urbain*, Economica, Paris, 1985.

[AYD 86] AYDALOT P. (ed.), *Milieux Innovateurs en Europe*, GREMI, Paris, 1986.

[AYR 96] AYRES R.U., "Le métabolisme industriel et les changements de l'environnement planétaire", *Revue internationale de sciences sociales*, vol. 121, pp. 401–412, 1996.

[BAI 77] BAIROCH P., *Taille des villes, conditions de vie et développement économique*, Editions de l'Ecole des hautes études en sciences sociales, Paris, 1977.

[BAR 11] BARREAU J.C., *Venise, un capitalisme à visage humain*, Fayard, Paris, 2011.

[BAT 13] BATTY M., *The New Science of Cities*, MIT Press, Cambridge, 2013.

[BET 13a] BETTENCOURT L., The kind of problem a city is, SFE working paper, 2013.

[BET 13b] BETTENCOURT L., The use of big data in smart cities, Santa Fé Institute working paper, 2013.

[BIH 10] BIHOUIX P., DE GUILLEBON B., *Quel futur pour les métaux ? Raréfaction des métaux : un nouveau défi pour la société*, EDP Sciences, 2010.

[BLA 70] BLACK R.D.C. (ed.), *The Theory of Political Economy*, Penguin, London, 1970.

[BOS 07] BOSCHMA R., FRITSCH M., "Creative class and regional growth – empirical evidence from eight European countries", *Jena Economic Research Papers*, 2007-066, 2007.

[BOU 03] BOUCHERON P., MENJOT D., *Histoire de l'Europe Urbaine*, vol. 2, Le Seuil, Paris, 2003.

[BRE 17] BREVILLE B., "Grandes villes et bons sentiments", *Le Monde Diplomatique*, November 2017.

[BRO 95] BROWNING L.D., BEYER J.M., SHELTER J.C., "Building cooperation in competitive industry: SEMATECH and the semiconductor industry", *Academy of Management Journal*, vol. 38, no. 1, pp. 113–151, 1995.

[BUD 16] BUDDS D., *5 Rules For Designing Great Cities, From Denmark's Star Urbanist*, available at: Fastcodesign.com, 2016.

[CAR 12] CARON F., *La dynamique de l'innovation*, Albin Michel, Paris, 2012.

[CGD 12] CGDD, "La ville intelligente : état des lieux et perspectives en France", *Etudes et Documents*, no. 73, Ministère de l'écologie, Paris, 2012.

[CHI 04] CHILES T.H., MEYER A.D., HENCH T.J., "Organizational emergence: the origin and transformation of Branson, Missouri's Musical Theaters", *Organization Science*, vol. 15, no. 5, pp. 499–519, September–October 2004.

[CIN 14] CINGANO F., Trends in income inequality and its impact on economic growth, OECD Social, Employment and Migration working papers, no. 163, OECD Publishing, Paris, 2014.

[CLE 16] CLERVAL A., *Paris sans le peuple, la gentrification de la capitale*, La Découverte, Paris, 2016.

[CLI 11] CLIMATE GROUP, Information Marketplaces: The New Economics of Cities, Report, 2011.

[COL 12] COLLETIS G., "Réindustrialiser la France par ses territoires", *Produire en France*, CNER, 2012.

[DED 84] DEDIJER S., *Au-delà de l'informatique, l'intelligence sociale*, Stock, Paris, 1984.

[DEL 17] DELANNOY I., *L'économie symbiotique*, Actes Sud, Arles, 2017.

[DEP 13] DEPARTMENT FOR BUSINESS, INNOVATION AND SKILLS, Research paper no. 136, London, 2013.

[DOU 15] DOULET J.-F., "L'urbanisme chinois et l'émergence du modèle "intégrationniste", *Métropolitiques*, available at: http://www.metropolitiques.eu /L-urbanisme-chinois-et-l- emergence.html, 27 April 2015.

[DUA 11] DUANY A., SPECK J., LYDON M. *et al.*, "The smart growth manual", *Sustainability: Science, Practice and Policy*, vol. 7, no. 2, pp. 89–90, 2011.

[DUB 48] DUBARLE P., *Le Monde*, 28 December 1948.

[DUB 14] DUBÉ S., "Qu'est-ce qu'un living Lab", *Living Labs White Book*, Montréal in vivo, Montreal, 2014.

[DUM 15] DUMONT G.F., "Les territoires dans la "mondialisation" : sur un trépied", *Population & Avenir*, no. 721, January–February 2015.

[DWO 14] DWOSKIN E., "How New York's Fire Department uses data mining", *Wall Street Journal*, 24 June 2014.

[ECK 12] ECKERT D., GROSSETTI M., MARTIN-BRELOT H., "La classe créative au secours des villes ?", *La vie des idées*, 28 February 2012.

[ELL 88] ELLUL J., *1912 – 1994, le bluff technologique*, Fayard, Paris, 1988.

[FLO 02] FLORIDA R., *The Rise of the Creative Class*, Basic Books, New York, 2002.

[FRE 95] FREEMAN C., "The national system of innovation in historical perspective", *Cambridge Journal of Economics*, vol. 19, no. 1, 1995.

[FRI 15] FRISON P., SEVATYANOVA O., *Novgorod ou la Russie oubliée*, Le Ver à Soie, 2015.

[FRO 89] FROSCH R., GALLOPOULOS N., "Des stratégies industrielles viables", *Pour la science*, vol. 145, pp. 106–115, 1989.

[FRO 15] FROST & SULLIVAN, Strategic Opportunity Analysis of the Global Smart City Market, Report, 2015.

[GAD 13] GADREY J., "Jérémy Rifkin, le gourou du Gotha européen", *Alternatives Economiques*, 12 May 2013.

[GAF 16] GAFFNEY C., ROBERTSON C., "Smarter than smart: Rio de Janeiro's flawed emergence as a smart city", *Journal of Urban Technology*, pp. 1–18, April 2016.

[GAL 58] GALBRAITH K., *The Affluent Society*, Houghton Mifflin HMH, Boston, 1958.

[GEH 13] GEHL J., *Pour des villes à échelle humaine*, Éditions Écosociété, Montreal, 2013.

[GEO 70] GEORGESCU ROEGEN N., *The Entropy Law and the Economic Process*, Harvard University Press, Cambridge, 1970.

[GER 62] GERSCHENKRON A., *Economic Backwardness in Historical Perspective*, Belknap Press, Cambridge, 1962.

[GER 15] GERSHENSON C., "Requisite variety, autopoiesis, and self-organization", *Kybernetes*, vol. 44, no. 6/7, pp. 866–873, 2015.

[GIL 15] GIL-GARCIA J. *et al.*, "What makes a city smart?", *Information Polity*, vol. 20, 2015.

[GIR 15] GIRAUD P.-N., *L'Homme inutile. Du bon usage de l'économie*, Odile Jacob, Paris, 2015.

[GOD 12] GODFREY P., "Architecting complex systems in new domains and problems: making sense of complexity and managing the unintended consequences", *Proceedings of Complex System and Design Management*, 2012.

[GOD 15] GODRON J., *La Tribune*, 31 March 2015.

[GOD 17] GODRON J., "Grand Paris: Réussir la métropole", *Revue des Anciens Elèves de l'ENA*, November 2017.

[GRE 13] GREENFIELD A., *Against the Smart City*, Kindle Edition, 2013.

[GRE 14] GREENWALD G., *Nulle part où se cacher*, JC Lattes, 2014.

[GUI 98] GUIZOT F., *General History of Civilization in Europe*, New York, 1898.

[GUI 14] GUILLUY C., *La France périphérique, Comment on a sacrifié les classes populaires*, Flammarion, Paris, 2014.

[GUI 16] GUILLUY C., *Le crépuscule de la France d'en haut*, Flammarion, Paris, 2016.

[HAL 17] HALL C., *Energy Return on Investment, A Unifying Principle for Biology, Economics, and Sustainability*, Springer, Berlin, 2017.

[HAR 68] HARDIN G., "The tragedy of the commons", *Science*, vol. 162, no. 3859, pp. 1243–1248, 13 December 1968.

[HAR 91] HARDY D., *From Garden Cities to New Towns: Campaigning for Town and Country Planning*, Taylor and Francis, Abington, 1991.

[HEE 90] HEERS J., *La ville au Moyen-Age en Occident*, Fayard, Paris 1990.

[HER 14] HERRMAN A.W., "Sustainable renewable energy: engineers' role in changing the built environment", in NATIONAL ACADEMY OF ENGINEERING (ed.), *Livable Cities of the Future*, National Academies Press, Washington, 2014.

[HEY 91] HEYLIGHEN F., "Modelling emergence", in KAMPIS G. (ed.), *World Futures: the Journal of General Evolution*, Special Issue on Creative Evolution, 1991.

[HEY 92] HEYLIGHEN F., "Distinction Dynamics: from mechanical to self-organizing evolution", in GINDEV E. (ed.), *Proceedings of the International Workshop "Analysis and Control of Dynamical Systems"*, CLCS, Bulgarian Academy of Sciences, Sofia, 1992.

[HEY 01] HEYLIGHEN F., JOSLIN C., "Cybernetics and second order cybernetics", in MEYERS R.A. (ed.), *Encyclopedia of Physical Science & Technology*, 3rd ed., Academic Press, New York, 2001.

[HOL 73] HOLLING C.S., "Resilience and stability of ecological systems", *Annual Review of Ecology and Systematics*, vol. 4, pp. 1–23, 1973.

[HOW 02] HOWARD E., *Garden Cities of Tomorrow*, 2nd ed., S. Sonnenschein & Co, London, 1902.

[HUR 13] HURDEBOURCQ P., L'innovation institutionnelle territoriale au service du développement économique: tentative de modélisation, PhD thesis, Aix Marseille University, November 2013.

[IDC 16] IDC, La transformation numérique du secteur de l'industrie : l'entreprise 4.0, du rêve à la réalité, Report, 2016.

[INF 16] INFOGROUP, Seattle tops Portland as most 'hipster' city in U.S., Report, available at: http://www.infogroup.com/defining-the-hippest-us-cities-infographic, 2016.

[JAC 61] JACOBS J., *Death and Life of Great American Cities*, Random House, New York, 1961.

[JAC 69] JACOBS J., *The Economy of Cities*, Random House, New York, 1969.

[JAC 85] JACOBS J., *Cities and the Wealth of Nations*, Random House, New York, 1985.

[JAM 11] JAMET P., "Fukushima a montré que l'improbable est possible", interview with Cécile Klingler, *La Recherche*, no. 453, June 2011.

[JAR 17] JARRIGE F., LE ROUX T., *La contamination du monde, une histoire des pollutions à l'âge industriel*, Le Seuil, Paris, 2017.

[KIR 14] KIRSANOVA N.Y., LENKOVETS O.M., "Solving monocities problem as a basis to improve the quality of life in Russia", *Life Science Journal*, vol. 11, no. 6s, pp. 522–525, 2014.

[KRO 09] KROB D., "Eléments d'architecture des systèmes complexes", in APPRIOU A. (ed.), *Gestion de la complexité et de l'information dans les grands systèmes critiques*, CNRS Editions, pp. 179–207, 2009.

[LAP 17] LAPORTE O., "Exigences écologiques et transformations de la société", *Cahiers français*, vol. 401, 2017.

[LEC 15] LE COURRIER DE RUSSIE, "Norilsk, Nord paradis", Interview, February 2015.

[LIC 09] LICHTENSTEIN B.B., PLOWMAN D.A., "The leadership of emergence: a complex systems leadership theory of emergence at successive organizational levels", *The Leadership Quarterly*, vol. 20, pp. 617–630, 2009.

[LIC 14] LICHTENSTEIN B., *Generative Emergence: A New Discipline of Organizational, Entrepreneurial, and Social Innovation*, Oxford University Press, New York City, 2014.

[LIS 46] LIST F., *Le système national d'économie politique*, Capelle, Paris, 1846.

[LIZ 12] LIZAROIU G.C., ROSCIA M., "Definition methodology for the smart cities model", *Energy*, vol. 47, pp. 326–332, 2012.

[LOO 03] LOO-LEE S. *et al.*, "Singapore's competitiveness as a global city", *Cities*, vol. 20, no. 2, pp. 115–127, 2003.

[MAH 10] MAHBUBANI K., "New Asian perspectives on governance", *Governance*, August 2010.

[MAN 13] MANIER B., *Un million de révolutions tranquilles*, Les Liens qui Libèrent, Paris, 2013.

[MAR 98] MARESCA B., Les villes de 100 000 à 200 000 habitants peuvent devenir les plus attractives, Research paper, CRÉDOC: Consommation et Modes de Vie Volume 138, 1998.

[MAR 17] MARKETSANDMARKETS, Smart Cities Market by Focus Areas, Transportation (Types, Solutions, Services), Utilities (Types, Solutions, Services), Buildings (Types, Solutions, Services), Citizen Services (Types), and Region - Global Forecast to 2022, Report, MarketsAndMarkets, 2017.

[MAT 13] MATHEWS J.A., "The renewable energies technology surge: a new techno-economic paradigm in the making?", *Futures*, vol. 46, pp. 10–22, 2013.

[MAT 14] MATHEWS J.A., REINERT E.S., "Renewables, manufacturing and green growth: energy strategies based on capturing increasing returns", *Futures*, vol. 61, pp. 13–22, 2014.

[MÉN 11] MÉNARD R., Dense Cities in 2050: the Energy Option?, ECEEE, 2011 Summer Study, 2011.

[MIC 13] MICHUN S. (ed.), "Actes du colloque Territoires, enjeux économiques et sociaux : quel engagement partagé des acteurs ? 6e Université d'été "Emploi, compétences, territoires"", *Relief*, no. 41, March 2013.

[MIL 00] MILLER R., *The Strategic Management of Large Engineering Projects: Shaping Institutions, Risks, and Governance*, MIT Press, Cambridge, 2000.

[MIN 15] MINISTERE DU TRAVAIL, DARES Analyses, Paris, November 2015.

[MIT 11] MITCHELL T., *Carbon Democracy*, Verso, London, 2011.

[MOK 02] MOKYR J., *The Gifts of Athena, the Historical Origins of the Knowledge Economy*, Princeton University Press, Princeton, 2002.

[MOO 65] MOORE G., *Electronics Magazine*, 19 April 1965.

[MOR 12] MOREL C., *Les décisions absurdes*. II, Gallimard, Paris, 2012.

[MOR 13] MOROZOV E., *To Save Eveything, Click Here*, Penguin, London, 2013.

[MUM 11] MUMFORD L., *La Cité à travers l'histoire*, Albin Michel, Paris, 2011.

[NEA 15] NEALER R., REICHMUTH D., ANAIR D., Cleaner Cars from Cradle to Grave: How Electric Cars Beat Gasoline Cars on Lifetime Global Warming Emissions, Union of Concerned Scientists, 2015.

[NEI 14] NEIROTTI P., DE MARCO A., CORINNA CAGLIANO A. *et al.*, "Current trends in Smart City initiatives: Some stylised facts", *Cities*, vol. 38, pp. 25–36, June 2014.

[NEW 98] NEWMAN P., KENWORTHY J., *Sustainability and Cities: Overcoming Automobile Dependence*, Island Press, Washington, 1998.

[OEC 14] OECD, Innovation-Driven Growth in Regions: The Role of Smart Specialisation, OECD, 2014.

[OEC 15] OECD, Programme Data-driven Innovation for Growth and Well-being, OECD, 2015.

[OST 91] OSTROM E., *Governing the Commons; The Evolution of Institutions for Collective Action*, Cambridge University Press, New York, 1991.

[OST 10] Ostrom E., "Beyond markets and states: polycentric governance of complex economic systems", *American Economic Review*, vol. 100, pp. 641–672, 2010.

[OST 14] Ostry J.D., Berg A., Tsangarides C., Redistribution, Inequality, and Growth, IMF, April 2014.

[OUR 16] Oury Diallo A., "Diamniado, l'ambitieux pari de Dakar", *Jeune Afrique*, 1 April 2016.

[PEC 07] Pecqueur B., "L'économie territoriale : une autre analyse de la globalisation", *L'Économie politique*, vol. 33, no. 1, pp. 41–52, 2007.

[PIT 18] Pitron G., *La guerre des métaux rares, la face cachée de la transition énergétique et numérique*, Les Liens qui Libèrent, Paris, 2018.

[POP 34] Popper K., *Logik der Forschung*, Mohr Siebeck, Heidelberg, 1934.

[PRU 17] Prud'homme R., *Le Mythe des énergies renouvelables : Quand on aime on ne compte pas*, L'Artilleur, 2017.

[REI 08] Reinert E., *How Rich Countries Got Rich and Why Poor Countries Stay Poor*, Anthem Press, London, 2008.

[REI 09] Reinert E.S., Rainer K., The Economics of Failed, Failing, and Fragile States: Productive Structure as the Missing Link, The Other Canon Foundation and Tallinn University of Technology working paper, TUT Ragnar Nurkse School of Innovation and Governance, 2009.

[REI 11] Reinert S.A. (ed.), *Antonia Serra, A Short Treatise on the Wealth and Poverty of Nations (1613)*, Anthem Press, London, 2011.

[REI 12] Reinert E.S., *Comment les pays riches sont devenus riches et pourquoi les pays pauvres restent pauvres*, Editions du Rocher, Monaco, 2012.

[REI 15] Reinert E.S., Mathews J.A., "Renewables, manufacturing and green growth: energy strategies based on capturing increasing returns", *Futures*, vol. 61, pp. 13–22, 2015.

[REI 16] Reinert S., *Antonio Serra and the Economics of Good Government*, Palgrave McMillan, London, 2016.

[ROB 90] Roberts K.H., "Some characteristics of one type of high-reliability organization", *Organization Science*, vol. 1, no. 2, pp. 160–176, 1990.

[ROC 08] Rochet C., "Le bien commun comme main invisible. Le legs de Machiavel à la gestion publique", *Revue Internationale des Sciences Administratives*, vol. 74, no. 3, pp. 529–553, 2008.

[ROC 10] ROCHET C., "Pas de philosophie, SVP, nous sommes des managers. Management public et bien commun : convergences euro-atlantiques", *Revue Internationale des Sciences Administratives*, vol. 76, no. 2, pp. 303–335, 2010.

[ROC 11a] ROCHET C., "Pour une logique de l'indiscipline – Réflexions sur l'éthique de la décision publique, autour du livre d'Alasdair Roberts. The Logic of Discipline", *Revue française d'administration publique*, vol. 2011/4, no. 140, pp. 723–737, 2011.

[ROC 11b] ROCHET C., *Qu'est-ce qu'une bonne décision publique?*, Editions Universitaires Européennes, Saarbrücken, 2011.

[ROC 14] ROCHET C., "L'Etat stratège, de la Renaissance à la troisième révolution industrielle", in TANNERY F., DENIS J.-P., HAFSI T. (eds), *Encyclopédie de la stratégie*, Vuibert, Paris, 2014.

[ROC 15a] ROCHET C., "Play it again, Sam", in *L'intelligence Iconomique*, De Boeck, Brussels, 2015.

[ROC 15b] ROCHET C., VOLLE M., *L'intelligence iconomique, les nouveaux modèles d'affaires de la III° revolution industrielle*, De Boeck Supérieur, Louvain, 2015.

[ROC 15c] ROCHET C., VOLLE M., *Les nouveaux modèles d'affaires de l'icononomie*, De Boeck Supérieur, Louvain, 2015.

[ROC 16a] ROCHET C., "Urban lifecycle management: system architecture applied to the conception and monitoring of smart cities", in AUVRAY G., BOCQUET J.C., BONJOUR E. *et al.* (eds), *Complex Systems Design & Management*, Springer, Cham, 2016.

[ROC 16b] ROCHET C., " L'état stratège face aux enjeux de l'iconomie", in GIAUQUE D. (ed.), *L'acteur et la bureaucratie au XXI° siècle*, IDHEAP, Lausanne, 2016.

[ROC 17a] ROCHET C., "Singapour, la voie des villes intelligentes", *Constructif*, vol. 46, 2017.

[ROC 17b] ROCHET C., BELEMLIH A., "Direct democracy as the keystone of a smart city governance as a complex system", in FANMUY G., GOUBAULT E., KROB D. *et al.* (eds), *Complex Systems Design & Management*, Springer, Cham, 2017.

[ROU 14] ROUVILLOIS F., *Crime et utopie, une nouvelle enquête sur le nazisme*, Flammarion, Paris, 2014.

[SAL 16] SALLIS J.F. *et al.*, "Physical activity in relation to urban environments in 14 cities worldwide: a cross-sectional study", *The Lancet*, vol. 387, no. 10034, pp. 2207–2217, 2016.

[SAS 12] SASSEN S., *Cities in a World Economy*, SAGE, London, 2012.

[SCH 10] SCHWARTZ H., *States vs Markets: The Emergence of a Global Economy*, Palgrave, London, 2010.

[SCH 12a] SCHMIDT E., Google's Eric Schmidt to graduates: 'Find a way to say YES to things', Public Affairs, UC Berkeley, 14 May 2012.

[SCH 12b] SCHAFFERS H., KOMNINOS N., PALLOT M. *et al.*, Smart Cities as Innovation Ecosystems Sustained by the Future of Internet, Fireball White paper, 2012.

[SIM 77] SIMON H., *Models of Discovery and Other Topics in the Methods of Science*, Springer, Heidelberg, 1977.

[SIM 96] SIMON H.A., *The Sciences of the Artificial*, 3rd ed., MIT Press, 1996.

[SIM 12] SIMONDON G., *Du mode d'existence des objets techniques*, Aubier, Paris, 2012.

[SIN 11] SINTOMER Y., *Petite histoire de l'expérimentation démocratique*, La Découverte, Paris, 2011.

[TAE 11] TAEWOO N., PARDO T.A., "Conceptualizing smart city with dimensions of technology, people, and institutions", *Proceedings of the 12th Annual International Conference on Digital Government Research*, 2011.

[TAI 88] TAINTER J., *The Collapse of Complex Societies*, Cambridge University Press, Cambridge, 1988.

[TOW 13] TOWNSEND A., *Smart Cities: Big Data, Civic Hackers, and the Quest for a New Utopia*, W.W. Norton & Company, New York, 2013.

[UND 13] UNDP and Institute for Environmental Studies, China Human Development Report: 2013, Sustainable and Liveable Cities: Toward Ecological Urbanisation, Chinese Academy of Social Sciences, 2013.

[URE 36] URE A., *Philosophie des manufactures, ou Économie industrielle de la fabrication du coton, de la laine, du lin et de la soie, avec la description des diverses machines employées dans les ateliers anglais*, L. Mathias, Paris, 1836.

[VAL 17] VALANTIN J.-M., *Géopolitique d'une planète déréglée*, Le Seuil, Paris, 2017.

[VAR 79] VARELA F., *Principles of Biological Autonomy*, Prentice Hall, Upper Saddle River, 1979.

[VEB 99] VEBLEN T., *The Theory of the Leisure Class*, Macmillan, London, 1899.

[VIC 00] VICHNIEVSKI A., *La faucille et le rouble : la modernisation conservatrice en URSS*, Gallimard, Paris, 2000.

[VON 42] VON THÜNEN J.H., *Der isolierte Staat in Beziehung auf Landwirtschaft und Nationalökonomie*, Fischer, Jena, 1842.

[VON 86] VON HIPPEL E., "Lead users: a source of novel product concepts", *Management Science*, vol. 32, no. 7, pp. 791–806, 1986.

[WAI 17] WAINWRIGHT O., "Everything is gentrification now: but Richard Florida isn't sorry", *The Guardian*, 26 October 2017.

[WEI 95] WEICK K.E., *Sensemaking in Organizations*, Sage, Thousand Oaks, 1995.

[WES 07] WEST G., BETTENCOURT L.M.A., LOBO J. *et al.*, "Growth, innovation, scaling, and the pace of life in cities", *PNAS*, vol. 104, no. 17, 2007.

[WIL 17] WILSON V., Racial inequality in wages, income and wealth show that MLK's work remains unfinished, Economic Policy Institute, 2017.

[ZIM 08] ZIMMERMAN J., "From brew town to cool town: Neoliberalism and the creative city development strategy in Milwaukee", *Cities*, vol. 25, pp. 230–242, 2008.

[ZOM 17a] ZOMBO M.-M., "L'écoefficacité : mieux gérer la gouvernance de l'eau potable au sud", Editions Universitaires Européennes, Saarbrücken, 2017.

[ZOM 17b] ZOMBO M.-M., "L'auto innovation sociale des pays en développement à l'export vers l'hexagone : management de l'entreprenariat en question", *Revue Africaine des Migrations Internationales*, vol. 1, no. 1, 2017.

[ZOM 17c] ZOMBO M.-M., L'écoefficacité : améliorer la gouvernance de l'eau potable en milieu rural des pays en développement, PhD thesis, Aix-Marseille University, February 2017.

Index

Other titles from

in

Information Systems, Web and Pervasive Computing

2018

ARDUIN Pierre-Emmanuel
Insider Threats
(Advances in Information Systems Set – Volume 10)

CHAMOUX Jean-Pierre
The Digital Era 1: Big Data Stakes

CARMÈS Maryse
Digital Organizations Manufacturing: Scripts, Performativity and
Semiopolitics
(Intellectual Technologies Set – Volume 5)

DOUAY Nicolas
Urban Planning in the Digital Age
(Intellectual Technologies Set – Volume 6)

FABRE Renaud, BENSOUSSAN Alain
The Digital Factory for Knowledge: Production and Validation of Scientific
Results

GAUDIN Thierry, LACROIX Dominique, MAUREL Marie-Christine, POMEROL
Jean-Charles
Life Sciences, Information Sciences

LIEM André
Prospective Ergonomics
(Human-Machine Interaction Set – Volume 4)

MARSAULT Xavier
Eco-generative Design for Early Stages of Architecture
(Architecture and Computer Science Set – Volume 1)

REYES-GARCIA Everardo
The Image-Interface: Graphical Supports for Visual Information
(Digital Tools and Uses Set – Volume 3)

REYES-GARCIA Everardo, BOUHAÏ Nasreddine
Designing Interactive Hypermedia Systems
(Digital Tools and Uses Set – Volume 2)

SAÏD Karim, BAHRI KORBI Fadia
Asymmetric Alliances and Information Systems:Issues and Prospects
(Advances in Information Systems Set – Volume 7)

SZONIECKY Samuel, BOUHAÏ Nasreddine
Collective Intelligence and Digital Archives: Towards Knowledge Ecosystems
(Digital Tools and Uses Set – Volume 1)

2016

BEN CHOUIKHA Mona
Organizational Design for Knowledge Management

BERTOLO David
Interactions on Digital Tablets in the Context of 3D Geometry Learning
(Human-Machine Interaction Set – Volume 2)

BOUVARD Patricia, SUZANNE Hervé
Collective Intelligence Development in Business

EL FALLAH SEGHROUCHNI Amal, ISHIKAWA Fuyuki, HÉRAULT Laurent, TOKUDA Hideyuki
Enablers for Smart Cities

FABRE Renaud, in collaboration with MESSERSCHMIDT-MARIET Quentin, HOLVOET Margot
New Challenges for Knowledge

GAUDIELLO Ilaria, ZIBETTI Elisabetta
Learning Robotics, with Robotics, by Robotics
(Human-Machine Interaction Set – Volume 3)

HENROTIN Joseph
The Art of War in the Network Age
(Intellectual Technologies Set – Volume 1)

KITAJIMA Munéo
Memory and Action Selection in Human–Machine Interaction
(Human–Machine Interaction Set – Volume 1)

LAGRAÑA Fernando
E-mail and Behavioral Changes: Uses and Misuses of Electronic Communications

LEIGNEL Jean-Louis, UNGARO Thierry, STAAR Adrien
Digital Transformation
(Advances in Information Systems Set – Volume 6)

NOYER Jean-Max
Transformation of Collective Intelligences
(Intellectual Technologies Set – Volume 2)

VENTRE Daniel
Information Warfare – 2nd edition

VITALIS André
The Uncertain Digital Revolution
(Computing and Connected Society Set – Volume 1)

2015

ARDUIN Pierre-Emmanuel, GRUNDSTEIN Michel, ROSENTHAL-SABROUX Camille
Information and Knowledge System
(Advances in Information Systems Set – Volume 2)

PLANTIN Jean-Christophe
Participatory Mapping

VENTRE Daniel
Chinese Cybersecurity and Defense

2013

BERNIK Igor
Cybercrime and Cyberwarfare

CAPET Philippe, DELAVALLADE Thomas
Information Evaluation

LEBRATY Jean-Fabrice, LOBRE-LEBRATY Katia
Crowdsourcing: One Step Beyond

SALLABERRY Christian
Geographical Information Retrieval in Textual Corpora

2012

BUCHER Bénédicte, LE BER Florence
Innovative Software Development in GIS

GAUSSIER Eric, YVON François
Textual Information Access

STOCKINGER Peter
Audiovisual Archives: Digital Text and Discourse Analysis

VENTRE Daniel
Cyber Conflict

2011

BANOS Arnaud, THÉVENIN Thomas
Geographical Information and Urban Transport Systems

DAUPHINÉ André
Fractal Geography

2009

BONNET Pierre, DETAVERNIER Jean-Michel, VAUQUIER Dominique
Sustainable IT Architecture: the Progressive Way of Overhauling Information Systems with SOA

PAPY Fabrice
Information Science

RIVARD François, ABOU HARB Georges, MERET Philippe
The Transverse Information System

ROCHE Stéphane, CARON Claude
Organizational Facets of GIS

2008

BRUGNOT Gérard
Spatial Management of Risks

FINKE Gerd
Operations Research and Networks

GUERMOND Yves
Modeling Process in Geography

KANEVSKI Michael
Advanced Mapping of Environmental Data

MANOUVRIER Bernard, LAURENT Ménard
Application Integration: EAI, B2B, BPM and SOA

PAPY Fabrice
Digital Libraries

2007

DOBESCH Hartwig, DUMOLARD Pierre, DYRAS Izabela
Spatial Interpolation for Climate Data

SANDERS Lena
Models in Spatial Analysis

2006

CLIQUET Gérard
Geomarketing

CORNIOU Jean-Pierre
Looking Back and Going Forward in IT

DEVILLERS Rodolphe, JEANSOULIN Robert
Fundamentals of Spatial Data Quality

Printed and bound by CPI Group (UK) Ltd, Croydon, CR0 4YY